# ARE YOU *(BIBLICALLY)* ORTHODOX?

### BY
### HARRISON L HAYS IV

*ENCOURAGEMENT INTL., INC.*

Northridge, CA
April 2022

Are You (Biblically) Orthodox? by Harrison Hays IV

© Harrison Hays IV
Encouragement International, Inc.
www.encouragementintl.com

All rights reserved. No part of this publication may be reproduced, or repurposed in any form by any means, electronic, mechanical, photocopy, recording, or otherwise, without the prior permission of the author except as allowed under fair use and United States copyright.

Cover design: Todd Shaffer

First printing 2023

Printed in the USA

ISBN: 979-8-9896375-1-5

## CONTENTS

**INTRODUCTION** .................................................................. 1

**CHAPTER ONE** ................................................................. 10

**CHAPTER TWO: THE NEED FOR JUSTIFICATION** .......... 15
    The Need For Justification ..................................................... 15
    Peace Through Justification ................................................... 17
    The Insufficiency of the Law For Justification ..................... 18
    Transformed from Sufficient to Insufficient ......................... 20

**CHAPTER THREE: THE MEANING OF JUSTIFICATION** . 22
    The Hebrew Term ................................................................. 22
    The Greek Term .................................................................... 23
    The Need to Define Monergism and Synergism .................. 24
    The Significance of Forensic Monergism ............................. 25
    The Source of Justification ................................................... 26
    Justification in the Gospels and the Book of Acts ................ 27
    Luke 18:9-14: An Important Prelude ................................... 27
    Understanding the Pharisees ................................................ 28
    Understanding the Tax Collectors ........................................ 28
    Understanding the Contrasts in the Parable ......................... 29
    The Lesson of the Parable .................................................... 29
    Gospel Conclusions .............................................................. 29
    A Clear Statement of Redemptive Justification in the Book of Acts ...................................................................................... 30
    A Challenge from the Book of James .................................. 31
    Paul's Support of Divine Monergistic Justification .............. 33

**CHAPTER FOUR: THE ROLE UNDERSTANDING IMPUTATION PLAYS IN DEFINING JUSTIFICATION** ...... 36

**CHAPTER FIVE: THE HISTORICAL REDEFINITION OF JUSTIFICATION** ............................................................... 42
    Justification to Chrystostom and Ambrosiaster ................... 43
    Justification to Augustine and Cyril of Alexandria .............. 45
    Justification According to Jerome ........................................ 57
    Justification to the Reformers .............................................. 60

  Justification Reintroduced to the Eastern Orthodox Church .... ........................................................................................................66
  Slavic Baptist Thinking on Justification Under the Influence of Eastern Orthodoxy .............................................................. 68
  Conclusion ............................................................................ 72

**CHAPTER SIX: THE EFFECT OF REDEFINING JUSTIFICATION** ................................................................... 75
  The Effect of Redefining Justification on Other Salvific Terms ..................................................................................... 75
  The Effect of Redefining Justification on the Understanding Of Salvation ........................................................................... 75
  The Effect of Redefining Justification on the Understanding of Sanctification And Salvation ......................................... 77
  Identifying Eastern Orthodox Theological Concepts in Slavic Baptist Thinking .................................................................. 81

**CHAPTER SEVEN: THE EFFECT OF REDEFINING JUSTIFICATION ON THE CONCEPT OF GRACE** ............... 83
  Grace .................................................................................... 83
  Preliminary Thoughts on the Eastern Orthodox Understanding of the Relationship between χάρις and δικαιοω ................... 86
  What Does Eastern Orthodoxy Mean by the *energies* of God? ............................................................................................. 91
  A Related Issue: Being Created in the Image and Likeness ................................................................................................ 92
  The Effect of Misunderstanding Justification, Grace, and of Being Created in the Image and Likeness of God on the Biblical Understanding of Faith ......................................... 99

**CHAPTER EIGHT: THE EFFECT OF REDEFINING JUSTIFICATIION ON THE CONCEPT OF FAITH** .............. 104

**CHAPTER NINE: THE EFFECT OF REDEFINING JUSTIFICATION ON THE CONCEPT OF SANCTIFICATION** ................................................................................................ 107

**CHAPTER TEN: THE THEOLOGICAL HISTORY OF THE CHURCH AND THE SLAVIC PROTESTANTS** ................... 114

    Eastern Orthodox History ...................................................... 114
    The Development of the Slavic Protestant Movement ...... 116
    Understanding Arminius and His Influence Among Slavic
    Baptists ..................................................................................... 120
    Theological Differences Between Some Slavic Baptists and
    The Eastern Orthodox ............................................................. 122

**CHAPTER ELEVEN: CONCLUSION** ........................................ 127
    A Challenge to My Reading Audience ............................... 128

**APPENDIX ONE: TABLE OF JUSTIFICATION USAGE IN THE NEW TESTAMENT** ....................................................... 129

**APPENDIX TWO: THE EFFECT OF REDEFINING JUSTIFICATION ON THE CONCEPT OF ELECTION** ....... 132
    Defining Election .................................................................... 132
    Does God Have a Bias in His Selection of Those He Will Elect
    to Redemption ......................................................................... 133

**APPENDIX THREE: THE EFFECT OF REDEFINING JUSTIFICATION ON THE CONCEPT OF ETERNAL SECURITY** ...................................................................................... 140
    Who Does Persevering Work? .............................................. 140
    Where Does the Bible Support This Concept of Sovereign
    Perseverance? .......................................................................... 141
    John 10:27-29 .......................................................................... 141
    2 Thessalonians 3:3 ................................................................ 144
    Romans 11:29 ......................................................................... 145
    Philippians 1:6 ........................................................................ 146
    1 Peter 1:5 ............................................................................... 146

**APPENDIX FOUR: TABLE OF COMPARISON** ................... 149

**ABOUT THE AUTHOR** ............................................................. 151

**BIBLIOGRAPHY** ........................................................................ 154

# ABBREVIATIONS

| | |
|---|---|
| ACCS | Ancient Christian Commentary on Scripture |
| ACT | *Ancient Christian Texts.* Thomas C. Oden and Gerald L Bray, editors. Downers Grove, IL: InterVarsity Press, 2009. |
| AUCECB | All Union Council of Evangelical Christians-Baptists |
| BDB | *The New Brown-Driver-Briggs-Genesius Hebrew and English Lexicon.* Peabody, MA: Hendrickson Publishers, 1979. |
| BECNT | Baker Exegetical Commentary on the New Testament |
| BST | The Bible Speaks Today |
| CJ | Concordia Journal |
| EAFUECB | Euro-Asian Federation of the Union of Evangelical Christians-Baptists |
| EDNTW | W. E. Vine, *Expository Dictionary of New Testament Words with Their Precise Meanings for English Readers.* Old Tappan, NJ: Revell, 1966. |
| ESV | English Standard Version |
| HTR | Harvard Theological Review |
| KJV | King James Version |
| LCC | Library of Christian Classics |
| MacNTC | MacArthur New Testament Commentary |
| MSJ | The Masters Seminary Journal |
| NASB | New American Standard Version |
| NICNT | New International Commentary on the New Testament |
| NICOT | New International Commentary on the Old Testament |
| NIDNTTE | *New International Dictionary of New Testament Theology and Exegesis* |

| | |
|---|---|
| NIDOTTE | *New International Dictionary of Old Testament Theology and Exegesis* |
| NIV | New International Version |
| NPNF | *Nicene and Post-Nicene Fathers.* Philip Schaff and Henry Wace, editors. Grand Rapids: Zondervan, 1975. |
| NTC | New Testament Commentary |
| REC | Reformed Expository Commentary |
| SECSA | Society of Evangelical Christians in the Spirit of the Apostles |
| TDNT | *Theological Dictionary of New Testament* |
| TNTC | Tyndale New Testament Commentary |
| UECB | Union of Evangelical Christians-Baptists |
| ZECNT | Zondervan Exegetical Commentary on the New Testament |
| ZPEB | *Zondervan Pictorial Encyclopedia of the Bible* |

# INTRODUCTION

*ARE YOU (BIBLICALLY) ORTHODOX?* is not just another theology book. It is a theology book that shows how redefining key theological terms has an adverse effect on Orthodox Biblical thinking. While Eastern Orthodox redefinition of key biblical terms is the primary focus of this book, this book will also enable one to see how the same definitional aberrations have also infiltrated Roman Catholicism in addition to some expressions of Protestantism.

The Eastern Orthodox Church uses the exact same terms and phrases that any evangelical Christian Church would use. However, the terms and phrases used by the Eastern Orthodox Church have drastically different meanings and definitions of key biblical terms with devastatingly different eternal results. The use of the terms "salvation" and "justification" by the Eastern Orthodox church (to take just two examples used in this book) are redefined in a way that results in the proclamation of what Paul would call a different Gospel in Galatians 1:6-9.

As a result, Eastern Orthodox (and Roman Catholic) theology since the fifth century has become nothing more than a system of works salvation dressed up to look like salvation by grace through faith. It is an illustration of Cain's efforts in Genesis 4:3 which was his religious exercise in trying to find favor with God according to his method. They both have the same results.

Words matter. Defining the terms correctly matters. This is especially true since defining words and terms relating to the gospel have eternal significance and determines who will enter the kingdom of heaven, whether a person's sins are forgiven, whether they will have their sins forgiven, will experience the New Birth, whether they will participate in the New Covenant, whether they will possess the new nature, and whether they will be baptized into the Body of Christ.

But defining biblical terms correctly not only ensures one's entrance into the Kingdom of God through the "narrow gate" but it also fosters growth and knowledge for understanding and advancing the gospel. Lack of knowledge and a proper understanding of biblical terminology has a devastating impact on God's people as evident in

Hosea 4:6 (My people are destroyed for lack of knowledge. Because you have rejected knowledge).

If defining terms and words are not important then Paul's exhortation to "rightly divide the Word of Truth" in 2 Timothy 2:15 is meaningless.

Our Lord Jesus Christ showed us how critical it is to properly define terms in order to understand the Scriptures. He did this when he refuted the Sadducees teaching on their understanding of "resurrection" in Matthew 22:31-32. In these verses Jesus showed that the two words "I AM" in the present tense establish His argument that there will be a resurrection in the future. He states:

> **31** "But regarding the resurrection of the dead, have you not read what was spoken to you by God: **32** 'I AM THE GOD OF ABRAHAM, AND THE GOD OF ISAAC, AND THE GOD OF JACOB '? He is not the God of the dead but of the living."

The Sadducee's did not believe in resurrection, heaven or life after death. Nor did they have a correct view of who God is in being the only true eternal God who has no part with anything related to death. Jesus teaches us that the correct use of two words made all the difference in the proper interpretation of Scripture on two of the most important subjects in all of Scripture—the resurrection and the eternality of God. The mouths of the Sadducees were shut as a result of correctly using and defining the words "I AM."

We find another example of how important it is to properly define biblical terms in John 10:22-42. This confrontation between Jesus and Jewish leaders happened a few months after the controversy described in John 9:1-10:21. The religious leaders were attempting to maneuver Jesus into making a statement where He would profess Himself to be the Messiah—a profession that they thought they could claim as blasphemy so they would, according to their thinking, have the justification to kill Him. Jesus, however, pointed out that His teachings and miracles were consistent with predictions of the coming Messiah (v25)—a defense which the religious leaders refused to accept about Him.

To further His defense, Jesus uses the same metaphors of the sheep and shepherd that He used after giving sight to a blind man (9:41-10:18) to carefully respond to their request (vv. 26-28). But He boldly closes the discussion with the claim that He and the Father are one (v.30). This statement by Jesus incited the Jewish leaders to respond with the intent to stone Him.

Jesus went on to back up this claim by using Scripture. Religious leaders and scribes of this era would often debate Scripture, using an endless barrage of technicalities and convoluted explanations to defend their position. Jesus engages them by citing Psalm 82 and specifically verse 6 which He claims is an Old Testament example for the grounds of His claim to be one with God. Jesus will compare a word used in Psalm 82:6 to establish that His claim to be Messiah is not blasphemous.

The one word He singles out is the word "gods" in 10:34 to claim it is not blasphemous for Him to claim to be God. In Psalm 82, God Himself calls men who function as judges' "gods". If "gods" is an appropriate description for those who are enabled to perform God's will as judges, then how can they (the Jewish religious leaders) stone Jesus (who has performed actual miracles as verifications of His Divine Messiahship) for blasphemy by claiming to be the Son of God? The religious leaders again were stumped once the proper definition of the word "gods" and the correct use of the term, as written in Scripture, was used.

Matthew 22:31-32 and John 10:22-42 are just two biblical examples showing the importance of using correct definitions of words in order to come to a proper theological, biblically orthodox conclusion. The Lord Jesus and the religious leaders of His time used the exact same words and terms. Yet they came to diametrically opposite conclusions and meanings.

It is interesting to note how in both instances Jesus, a Divine member of the Trinity who authored the Scriptures, used Scripture for His defense as He corrects sinful men in their understanding of Divine truth. While His arguments are conclusive and the correct interpretation which the religious leaders cannot argue against, they refuse to alter their condemnatory conclusion against Him.

Terms, words and how they are defined are eternally significant on how they are used and defined. It is clear that sinful man, unless guided by the Holy Spirit and a correct interpretation of Scripture, will always take something "holy," like the Law or Scripture, and twist and pervert it to mean something it was never meant to say or even imply.

The religious leaders, in Jesus' time, perverted and defined terms and words wrongly as Jesus pointed out over and over again. Sadly, the Eastern Orthodox, Roman Catholics and some Protestants have used the same terms and words which biblical Christianity uses but with completely different meanings and definitions. Eternal damnation waits for those who hold to such heresies. Thus, we must be vigilant in making certain that we define terms and words in the way that the Scriptures meant them to be defined.

The Table of Comparisons below shows how the exact same word, or terminology can be used by the Eastern Orthodox, the Roman Catholic and Arminian theologians with incorrect definitions of biblical terms to result in a contrary understanding of Scripture.

## Table of Comparisons

|  | Bible | Eastern Orthodoxy | Roman Catholicism | Arminian Theology |
|---|---|---|---|---|
| Justification | Reckoned by Forensic Declaration | Forensic fiction Fused with Sanctification | Fused with Sanctification | Forensic declaration Fused with Sanctification |
| Justification | Divine monergism | Divine initiation Human completion | Divine initiation Human completion | Divine initiation Human completion |
| Imputation | Reckoned | Infused Process | Infused Process | Infused Process |
| Salvation Past | Divine monergism Penalty of sin fully paid | Divine Initiation | Divine Initiation | Divine Initiation |

| | | | | |
|---|---|---|---|---|
| Salvation Present | Synergism Power of sin is broken in the redeemed | synergism | synergism | synergism |
| Salvation Future | Divine monergism (glorification) Presence of sin finally removed | Continuing synergistic process | Continuing synergistic process | Divine Monergistic reward |
| Sanctification Past | Positional Monergism Penalty of sin is fully paid | Infused at justification | Infused at justification | Infused at justification |
| Sanctification Present | Progressive synergism Power of sin is broken in the redeemed | Human emphasized synergism (theosis) | Human emphasized synergism | Human emphasized synergism |
| Sanctification Future | Perfected monergism Presence of sin is finally removed | Eternal synergistic effort (theosis) | Eternal synergistic effort | Divine monergistic reward |
| Grace | Monergistic favor | Synergistic energies of God | Conditional Divine Favor | Synergistic favor |
| Faith | Monergistic confidence | Synergistic confidence | Synergistic insecurity | Synergistic insecurity |
| Image of God | Structural Character | Propensity to seek perfection | Structural Character | Structural Character |
| Likeness of God | Structural Character | Perfection accomplished with great effort | Structural Character | Structural Character |
| Election | Divine Monergistic selection | Divine confirmation of human selection | Divine Confirmation of Human selection | Monergistic foreknowledge |
| Perseverance | Monergistic effort | Synergistic work | Synergistic work | Synergistic effort |

No wonder it can be so confusing for the average church goer or person seeking to follow Jesus Christ. And why it is so important for definitions—exact definitions—to be provided when we teach God's Word. The distinctions, and differences provided in the Table of Comparisons show that all four theological positions cannot be right and that there are eternal consequences for getting it wrong. Terms such as "justification," "grace," "faith," "sanctification" and "salvation" all need to be correctly defined and properly taught as the Scriptures teach them.

Every book, movie and song have a thesis statement. It is upon that thesis statement that everything in the book, movie or song will be built. If one looks for the thesis statement, it will become apparent what the writer or director is trying to say or prove. The Apostle John had a thesis statement when he wrote in John 20:30-31:

> *"30 And many other signs truly did Jesus in the presence of his disciples, which are not written in this book. 31 But these are written, that ye might believe that Jesus is the Christ, the Son of God; and that believing ye might have life through his name."*

From John's thesis statement, he proved that Jesus was the Christ, the Son of God, by showing His claims to be the Christ, the Son of God, in His nine "I AM" statements (John 6:35,41,48,51; 8:12; 8:58; 9:5; 10:7,9; 10:11,14; 11:25;14:26; 18:4,5) and in the seven signs Jesus did showing His sovereignty and power in His miracles of healing, nature, power over demonic forces and in creating only as God could (John 2:11; 4:46 – 54; 5:1-18; 6:1-14; 6:15-25; 9:1 – 41; 11:1 – 46).

Isaiah's thesis statement is that "God is a Holy God, and He expresses that holiness in judgment (Chapters 1 – 39) and in salvation (Chapters 40 – 66). Obadiah's thesis statement is that "God humbles and judges the proud."  Matthew's thesis statement is "Jesus is the Prophesied Messiah."  Luke's thesis statement, throughout the Gospel of Luke and the book of Acts, is that "God's promised salvation, via the Davidic Covenant, is for the Jews first and then the

Gentiles."

In each of these examples, the thesis statement is the spine to the entire book. It shows what the purpose of the author is and how each part fits into what the purpose is. Every book in the Bible has a thesis statement. And from it, how all the parts fit together in this book historically and theologically.

These examples also show how important terms and properly defined words are to a proper understanding of Scripture. This is the thesis statement *of "ARE YOU (BIBLICALLY) ORTHODOX?."* And all of its chapters flow from this thesis statement question.

- Chapter 2 shows the need for "justification" by sinful man.
- In Chapter 3, the word "justification" is defined as the Bible defines it.
- Chapter 4 the role and definition of how God's salvation is imparted to sinful man is shown. The Biblical understanding of "imputation" is discussed and how Eastern Orthodoxy and Roman Catholicism twists the Biblical view of "imputation."
- In Chapter 5, a historical overview is given to show the cultural and theological reasons why there was a redefinition of "justification". It is a warning to all of us not to allow historical events or culture define what the Scriptures teach.
- Chapter 6 will show the impact and the effect that redefining the word "justification" had, and continues to have, in Eastern Orthodoxy on understanding terminology regarding salvation. The result is a "different Gospel" which is anathema in the eyes of the Scriptures.
- Chapter 7 then shows how redefining "justification" and "sanctification" impacts the definition of "grace". The redefinition is no longer "God's unmerited favor to sinful man" but now a mix of "God's grace and human works" combined to gain God's grace and salvation. Justification and Sanctification are terms

that are now confused and combined to mean something that is completely foreign to the Gospel of Jesus Christ.
- Chapters 8 and 9 deal with the ripple effect that such redefinitions have on the terms "Faith" and "Sanctification". The "Gospel" becomes unrecognizable and becomes nothing more than a "works righteousness" now that "justification" and "grace" have been redefined.
- Chapter 10 gives a historical overview of the Eastern Orthodox Church and its influence on the Slavic Protestant Movement and how Arminian Theology came to replace the original thinking of Slavic Baptists on sovereign grace in salvation.
- Appendix #1 is a Table showing how "justification" is used in the New Testament. In this Appendix, it becomes clear that biblical "justification" is NOT used in the manner that the Eastern Orthodox, or the Roman Catholic Church, uses the term. A clear definition becomes evident which shows that Eastern Orthodox theology is a "different Gospel" than the one proclaimed in the Scriptures.
- Appendices #2 and #3 deal with the doctrines of "election" and "eternal security", and how that impacts the teaching of Eastern Orthodoxy. It shows the primary aspect of salvation being the work of God and not a mix of "grace" and "works" as Eastern Orthodoxy teaches.

As one reads *ARE YOU (BIBLICALLY) ORTHODOX?* you might be challenged by your own theological understanding in these areas and realize you had no idea that what you believe is not only diametrically opposed to Biblical Orthodox Christianity but might possibly be heretical.

We live in a culture where gender is fluid, where words are constantly being redefined to mean the exact opposite of what they have historically meant, where terms no longer have any definitive meaning, where terms are renamed so they hurt people's feelings less and where words have no absolute meaning so everyone can be included into God's Kingdom. It is exactly what Isaiah stated his culture was like in Isaiah 5:20. And the end result of that type of relativistic culture and ritualistic religion was nothing but swift and complete judgment by YHWH.

Words have definitions and meanings that communicate a concept and a message. What one believes is defined by what they believe about the Bible which is often referred to as "The Word of God." What one believes about "The Word" is dependent on how one defines the words in "The Word."

Prayerfully, this book will stretch your understanding, challenge your preconceived ideas and force you to choose what you believe and why you believe what you believe. And that is how it should be. Jesus said as much when He stated that "I am the truth"…..and that "truth" has only one meaning or the Word of God is nothing but a relativistic book with pious platitudes which mean nothing.

# CHAPTER ONE

## ARE YOU *(BIBLICALLY)* ORTHODOX?

Early in His ministry, around 28 AD, Jesus warned His followers to be on the lookout for false prophets (Matt 7:15). He said they would come looking as innocent as sheep but inwardly are ravenous wolves. The Apostle Paul, around 55 AD, also warned that false prophets would soon be infiltrating the Ephesian church (Acts 20: 28-30) and that the church leaders (the *elders*) should be on guard to protect their flock from the false teacher's seemingly innocent but destructive teaching which they would attempt to introduce into the church. Peter, around 68 AD, warned his audience that false teachers were coming (2 Pet 2:1) and were bringing with them "destructive heresies". Jude, not long after 2 Peter was written (also around 68 AD), warned that false teachers were now in the church (Jude 1:4). Over twenty-five years later, around 95 AD, the Apostle John was writing to deal with the infiltration of false teachers within the Ephesian church who were intent on deceiving those in Ephesus (1 John 4:1-7). Thus, beginning with the warnings by Jesus, the church had time to prepare for the onslaught of destructive heresies these false teachers would attempt to establish as acceptable ideas in the church of Jesus Christ.

Not surprisingly, these false prophets and false teachers attack the fundamental doctrine of Jesus' church. This fundamental teaching involves the Person and work of Jesus It comes attacking the Humanity and Divinity of Jesus as well as the sufficiency of His work on the cross.

Jesus, Paul, Peter, Jude and John had strong words of denunciation for false teachers and false prophets. Paul used especially hostile language on false teachers. In Galatians 1:6-9, he cursed anyone attempting to alter the gospel message that diminishes the sufficiency and way of acquiring the benefits of Jesus' work on the cross. Paul especially emphasized that anyone proclaiming a gospel that added to the work of Christ on the cross was cursed by God (Gal 2:16). The benefit of the gospel, according to Jesus and the writers of the New Testament, was received through 100% faith (confidence) in the complete and sufficient work of Jesus on the cross—man cannot add to the work of Jesus to find favor with God. Jesus' work alone on the cross was sufficient to restore the relationship with God that was lost through the sin of Eve and Adam in the Garden.

This gospel has been under attack since it was revealed by God to the world. It has always been endangered by Satan and his cohorts—in both the spiritual and natural world. Since the gospel is endangered, it is all the more important in these last days to make certain that those who claim to represent God are proclaiming the one true gospel.

During the church age, the gospel will be proclaimed through men (Matt 28:19–20). But, like tares among the wheat, false teachers (tares) will appear to look like God's true teachers (wheat). Therefore, it is imperative that our understanding of the gospel come from a source outside of man.

If we are to properly evaluate the gospel message to distinguish between true and false teachers of the gospel, we must begin with an authoritative source. When that authoritative source is dependent upon men properly but verbally transmitting this message from age to age there is the danger of communicating a misunderstood or improperly conveyed gospel. When this misunderstood or improperly conveyed message becomes tradition and is propagated as being true based on the authority of men, then countless souls for eternity are at stake.

God has not left His message in the "hands" of men alone (John 2:24,25). Rather, He has left His authority in His written word with the intention that His true teachers and messengers would derive their understanding of His message from His revelation which He has carefully preserved through the ages. The sixty-six books of the Bible—and *ONLY* the sixty-six books of the Bible— are His well-preserved revelation containing His message to man. Each generation of God's gospel messengers must base their understanding of the gospel on the authority of God's revelation found *only* in the Bible. If they base their understanding on the authority of tradition from the previous generation, there is danger of an improper and misunderstood message being communicated because the words being used to communicate that message may not be properly defined or understood by the next generation. The proper definition of the terms used by God in His revelation reduces or eliminates the misunderstanding of God's preserved revelation in the Bible.

The proper understanding of the gospel since it was delivered by Christ and the Apostles almost 2,000 years ago is being distorted today by the improper transmission through the tradition of those calling themselves authoritative leaders in the Church. The Roman Catholic church and the Eastern Orthodox church have a gospel tradition that has not been faithful to God's revelation as preserved in the Bible. This unfaithfulness is the result of abandoning a lexically based definition of God's word and replacing it with philosophically defined definitions. The book in your hands will examine the gospel with the starting point that is based upon proper Hebrew and Greek definitions of key theological terms (salvation, grace, faith, justification, sanctification and glorification with justification being the key theological concept for understanding the gospel). Once the proper definitions are in place, this book will trace how philosophical definitions during previous generations replaced the proper understanding of these key terms describing the spiritual birth. The result has been an anathematized gospel. The foundation of this study, then, centers upon a proper understanding of what it means to be justified before God.

Justification by faith alone is rightly considered the hallmark of the Reformation.[1] Luther, in his struggle for reconciliation with God from the effects of sin, found solace only after understanding and embracing the biblical teaching of justification by faith alone.[2] It was the primary issue of the other Reformers as well. John Calvin called

---

[1] James Buchanan, *The Doctrine of Justification* (Grand Rapids: Baker, 1997), vii.

[2] Roland H. Bainton, *Here I Stand: A Life of Martin Luther* (Nashville: Abingdon-Cokesbury Press, 1950), 48.

justification "the main hinge on which all religion turns."[3] Justification is so important to Christian thought that Wayne Grudem has said, "If we are to safeguard the truth of the gospel for future generations, we must understand the truth of justification."[4] This doctrine is so important that an improper understanding of the term affects salvation and one's eternal destiny as well as one's practical sanctification and everyday pursuit of a lifestyle pleasing to God. Most importantly, it either exalts or demeans the glory of God.

Understanding and describing justification, and the relationship between faith and works has been and is a struggle among the various groups identifying themselves as the true church. It was a struggle in the first century, as evidenced in the writings of Paul and James, and the struggle continues today. There are three primary streams of thought regarding justification: Roman Catholicism, Eastern Orthodoxy, and Protestantism. While the Roman Catholic and Eastern Orthodox churches at one time had a uniform understanding of justification, they now diverge. Protestants began with a unified understanding of justification but have developed variations in their understanding of the term since the Reformation.

When did the Eastern Orthodox and Roman Catholics depart from a biblical understanding of justification? Why did the Reformers return to a biblical understanding on justification? When the Slavic Baptist movement began in the 1800's, were they Reformed in their understanding of justification? Is the modern-day Slavic Baptist movement faithful to its original understanding of justification? Does the Eastern Orthodox understanding of salvation influence the Slavic Baptist understanding of salvation? These are all questions that will be dealt with in this book.

To accomplish this task will require biblical definitions of justification, salvation, faith, and sanctification because understanding these terms closely interwoven in the regenerative

---

[3] John Calvin, *Institutes of the Christian Religion* (repr., Peabody, MA: Hendrickson Publishers, 2008), 3.11.1.

[4] Grudem, *Systematic Theology*, 722.

work of God and are defined differently by Protestants, Roman Catholics, the Eastern Orthodox and among some Protestant groups. Poor and improper definitions of these terms have led to a faulty understanding of justification and grace throughout church history. Regrettably, this faulty understanding shows up in Protestant thinking as well.

# CHAPTER TWO
## THE NEED FOR JUSTIFICATION

**The Need For Justification**

In his book *Knowing God*, Anglican theologian J. I. Packer asks a thought-provoking question: "What is the best thing in life, bringing more joy, delight, and contentment, than anything else?" His answer is "the knowledge of God."[5] He proves his point by quoting Jer 9:23–24a, "Thus says the LORD, 'Let not a wise man boast of his wisdom, and let not the mighty man boast of his might, nor let a rich man boast of his riches: but let him who boasts boast of this, that he understands and knows Me." Rather than being just an answer to a thought-provoking question from an inquiring and intelligent man, YHWH expresses His desire for man to pursue the knowledge of Himself! Better yet, YHWH tells His people that knowing Him will bring them immense joy! He wants His creation to know Him.

Eastern Orthodox theologian Bishop Kallistos of Diokleia posits an equally thought-provoking question: "How can humans know an unknowable God?"[6] He goes on to give an elaborate explanation of how the unknowable Creator can become known by those He created.

But Ware's question prompts another question: "Why is God unknowable?" There are several responses that one could give. God is unknowable because He is transcendently intelligent. Isaiah 55:8–9 says, "'For My thoughts are not your thoughts, neither are your ways my ways,' declares the LORD. 'For as the heavens are higher than the earth, so are My ways higher than your ways, And My thoughts than your thoughts.'"

God is unknowable also because He is transcendently spiritual in contrast to humanity's limiting materiality. John 4:24 explains that God is Spirit, and that man has the need to become spiritual in order to worship Him.

But more importantly, God is unknowable because He is

---

[5] J. I. Packer, *Knowing God* (Downers Grove, IL: InterVarsity, 1973), 29.

[6] Ware, *The Orthodox Church*, 67.

transcendently holy. In Exodus 15:11, Moses leads the nation of Israel in singing, "Who is like You among the gods, O LORD? Who is like You, majestic in holiness, awesome in praises, working wonders?" In 1 Sam 2:2, Hannah prays, "There is no one holy like the LORD, indeed there is no one besides You, nor is there any rock like our God."

God's transcendent holiness was not an issue with His creation initially. When God made Adam and Eve and placed them in the Garden of Eden, Genesis 3:8 tells us that God was in the habit of making Himself known to them in the cool of the day. They were holy as evidenced by God walking with them in the cool of the day and being at peace with them. He enjoyed knowing Adam and Eve as well as fellowshipping with them. It was an unhindered, natural, and perfect relationship.

But knowing God, walking with God, and being at peace with God took a dramatic change when Adam and Eve rebelled against God by eating the forbidden fruit (Gen 3:6). The consequence, recorded in Genesis 3:24, was that God drove Adam and Eve from the Garden—the place where God was knowable and walking in peace with His creation. As a consequence of Adam and Eve's rebellion to God's standard, God no longer permitted His creation to possess intimate knowledge of Him—a knowledge for which they were designed to receive and use in the worship of Him. God was now at enmity with man.[7] As John Murray has well said, there was a disruption of relations between God and men.[8]

In order to restore fellowship with man, God must provide a way for making peace with man. Man is not able to initiate peace with God because such an effort would be originating from an imperfect or sinful man and God has made clear that such an effort is woefully deficient in His eyes (Isa 64:6). From God's perspective, man is incapable of knowing the way to make peace with Him (Isa 59:8). God must initiate the effort to make peace with man in order to restore

---

[7] Bruce Demarest, *The Cross and Salvation* (Wheaton, IL: Crossway, 2006), 66.

[8] Murray, *Redemption Accomplished and Applied*, 29.

the privilege of walking with intimate knowledge of Him. God's effort must be sufficient to bring about peace with mankind and nothing can be added to His effort once it has been accomplished so that the glory of His work will not be diminished.

Both Packer and Ware present a peace plan for knowing God in their books. Both authors go on to acknowledge the need for a bridge between God and His creation to accomplish this goal. That bridge is the person and work of Jesus the Christ. But one author builds his case for knowing and making peace with God on faith in Jesus' work alone while the other builds his case on faith in Jesus' work as a starting point that must be completed through one's own works. Both call themselves Christian. They share the same pursuit—being at peace with and being known by God. But the two could not be more diametrically opposed on the means by which peace and knowledge are obtained. Packer asserts that the Bible teaches faith alone as the foundation for being at peace with and being known by God. Conversely, Ware asserts that the Bible teaches faith plus performing works over the space of eternity will produce peace with and knowledge by God. Which is the true, biblically orthodox teaching?

## Peace Through Justification

Can a man's works accomplish the quest to find peace with God and restore the intimate fellowship with God that was lost at the Fall? The Apostle Paul has a definitive answer to this question. In Romans 5:1, Paul proclaims that justification through faith *ALONE* is the only means by which a person can be at peace with God. Prior to this claim, Paul in two statements establishes that faith *alone* in God's work justifies a man before God (Rom 3:20, 28). These are in addition to four statements he had made less than a decade earlier to the Galatian churches (Gal 2:16; 3:2, 5, 10). Therefore, efforts initiated and performed by man can neither result in peace nor restore intimate fellowship with God. Only faith in the sufficiency of Jesus' work on the cross can result in peace and restore intimate fellowship with God that was lost by the disobedience of Eve and Adam.

In each passage above, Paul contrasts being justified by God through faith with being justified by God through works. Each time he references works, he qualifies it as "works of the law" (ἔργων νόμου).[9] A work (ἔργον) is the accomplishment of a task, a duty, an assignment, or an obligation. Paul declares that the accomplishment of the task or obligation to which he is referencing is defined by the Law of God. But he also says that pursuing works of the Law as the means to be justified is an impossible task (Gal 2:16).

## The Insufficiency of the Law for Justification

To show the shortcomings of the Law as a means of restoring peace with God, Paul poses a question in Gal 3:2: "This is the only thing I want to find out from you; did you receive the Spirit by works of the Law, or by hearing with faith?" He goes on to say adversely in Galatians 3:10 that works of the law cannot accomplish this task ("For as many as are the works of the Law are under a curse; for it is written, 'Cursed is everyone who does not abide by all things written in the book of the law, to perform them.'") Paul makes this last point by appealing to his understanding of Deut 27:26. The foundational truth he asserts is clear—works cannot accomplish what only faith is able to do. This is true because breaking the Law just one time is equivalent in God's eyes to complete and absolute failure—a failure that man cannot overcome through his own effort! As Jas 2:10 states, "For whoever keeps the whole law and yet stumbles in one point, he has become guilty of all."

What is the Law that Paul and Moses are referring to? It is a set of standards or instructions initiated as a covenant by the divine, sovereign God on behalf of His vassal-people detailing how to live in a knowledgeable relationship with Him.[10] As Murray notes, the Law "has both penal sanctions and positive demands."[11] As the sovereign over His creation, His Law requires obedience and when there is *dis*obedience it is deemed as rebellion against His sovereign will and

---

[9] W. E. Vine, "Work", *EDNTW* (Old Tappan, NJ: Fleming H. Revell, 1966), 4:231.

[10] William Barrick, "The Mosaic Covenant," *MSJ* 10, no. 2 (Fall 1999), 215.

[11] Murray, *Redemption Accomplished and Applied*, 17.

requires justice.[12]

Justice is giving what is deserved. Justice for obedience brings a blessing. Justice for *dis*obedience deserves a consequence. In the case of disobedience, the consequence is a curse, that is, something that causes harm or injury. In Galatians 3:10, the word for curse (ἐπικατάρατος) is a compound word meaning an utterance of malevolence spoken against another.[13] In this case, it is a statement of condemnation uttered by God against those who fail to obey His Law. More simply put by way of contrast, obedience to the Law brings blessing (see Deut 28:1-14) while disobedience to the Law causes harm and is condemned (i.e., is cursed) by God.

The Law lacks compassion once disobedience has occurred. It is unmoved by a person's obedience to correct the wrong that has been done. The Law also does not rejoice at obedience, nor does it sorrow over disobedience. It is an objective code or a set of instructions which reflect the character of God that He uses to measure obedience and identify disobedience (Rom 7:12; 1 Tim 1:8). Since the Law is grounded in the God's character, its code or instructions are inflexible and cannot tolerate any deviation.

The Law is not only un-moved by a person's disobedience, but it is unemotional as well because it is a set of instructions lacking personality and feelings. It has no capacity for compassion or sympathy for obedience or disobedience. It is also exacting because it does not tolerate disobedience. The Law, since it is grounded in the character of God, expects perfection. Anything less than perfect obedience to the Law of God is cursed, condemned, and results in harm by God to the violator.[14] Adam and Eve experienced God's cursing, condemnation and harm which they were unable to overcome

---

[12] Barrick, "The Mosaic Covenant," 228.

[13] *EDNTW*, "Curse," 1:262–63.

[14] *The Curse of the Law* (gty.org, 1992), https://www.gty.org/library/sermons-library/80-105/the-curse-of-the-law. MacArthur gives a quick message describing the utter despair that comes from trying to obey the Law of God.

through their own efforts. Even their feeble attempt to cover the shame of their nakedness was replaced by a better solution initiated by God. God's perfect righteousness demands nothing less.

## Transformed From Sufficient to Insufficient

Adam was not created condemned by God; he became condemned by God. George Zemek quotes E. J. Young's description of Adam's unique experience: "When Adam sinned, he fell from an estate of being good into an estate of being evil."[15] He went from being "very good" into a state of sin and misery. His sin plunged him and his progeny into enmity with God. By contrast, his progeny did not become condemned, they were born condemned (Pss 51:5; 58:3; Gen 6:5; 8:21; Job 15:14; Jer 17:9). Adam introduced sin into humanity's existence while we, as Adam's progeny, perpetuate the existence of sin.[16] Thus, the sons of Adam enter the world in need of a justice that satisfies their cursed condition with its condemnation before God. As unredeemed man ages, he continually demonstrates his certain, eternal condemnation for disobedience to God's standards. Justice will only be satisfied, and peace only obtained with God when the condemned are justly sentenced and the just sentence for disobedience is conducted.

Revelation 20:11–15 describes the courtroom scene where final justice is meted out. Verse 12 describes books by which a just God judges His creation. The one who advances into an eternity of suffering does so because his name is not found in the Book of Life( Rev 20:12,15).[17] As MacArthur notes, the imagery reminds one of a citizenship registry in ancient cities. You were a citizen of the city if your name was registered in the city books. In the same way, you are

---

[15] George J. Zemek, *A Biblical Theology of the Doctrines of Sovereign Grace* (Little Rock, AR: B. T. D. S. G., 2002), 86. Zemek quotes from E. J. Young, *Genesis 3* (London: Banner of Truth, 1966), 60.

[16] Demarest, *The Cross and Salvation,* 73.

[17] John MacArthur, *Revelation 12-22*, MacNTC (Chicago: Moody Press, 2000), 255.

a citizen of heaven if your name is registered in the heavenly book, the Book of Life.

The one whose name is not written in the Book of Life will find himself evaluated by God according to his deeds (ἔργον). As Walvoord points out, it is dangerous to be evaluated according to your deeds.[18] In Rev 2:23, a statement of judgment is proclaimed against the deeds of the unrepentant who were associating with the church of Thyatira. In Rev 18:3–6, it is a statement of judgment against the deeds of the unredeemed. In Rev 20:11–15, it is a statement of judgment against the deeds of those whose name is not written in the Book of Life.

Revelation 20:15 is an important verse because it shows that no man will enter into eternity at peace and knowing God as a result of being able to satisfy the justice of God by performing deeds or works. Instead, his or her name must be *justifiably* written in the Book of Life to avoid eternal suffering.

How does a person find his name *justifiably* written in the Book of Life? How is justice accomplished for someone who is condemned by the Law of God? The answer is found in the gospel message. A man is justified through faith alone in the work of God (cf. Rom 4:3, Gal 3:6, and Gen 15:6). What it means to be justified, then, is important to understand. But, as will be demonstrated, the biblical definition of justification has been modified by some, altering man's understanding of redemption as New Testament history has progressed.

---

[18] John F. Walvoord, *The Revelation of Jesus Christ* (Chicago: Moody Press, 1966), 307.

# CHAPTER THREE

## THE MEANING OF JUSTIFICATION

### Justification: The Lexical Foundation

The word group for justification and righteousness in both the Hebrew and the Greek come from the same root which expresses a legal or forensic meaning.[19] In the Hebrew, צַדִּיק means the standard used by God to maintain order in this world.[20] This can be seen in Ps 5:12; 7:10–11; Prov 3:33; Jer 20:12; and Ezek 3:20–21.[21] It is not so much an ethical term as it is a *forensic* term.

### The Hebrew Term

The term forensic describes the legally binding action of a judge to decide and declare his decision to all parties in a courtroom setting. As Morris states, צַדִּיק "makes its home in the law of God."[22] He notes that the word's forensic nature is established in Gen 18:25 where Abraham describes God with the legal term, 'Judge' and thus men could depend upon YHWH to act consistently in righteousness (דִּיק) in contrast to heathen gods who acted capriciously.[23]

Deuteronomy 25:1 links forensic judgment and justification. Judgment is the legal process of resolving a dispute when one party charges the other with wrongdoing. When the judge renders his legal verdict in the dispute, his verdict is a legal declaration of righteousness in favor of one party.[24] Both Murray[25] and Morris[26] state

---

[19] Leon Morris, *The Apostolic Preaching of the Cross* (Grand Rapids: Eerdmans, 1976), 259.

[20] Morris., 259.

[21] *BDB*, "צַדִּיק," 843.

[22] Morris, *The Apostolic Preaching of the Cross,* 261.

[23] Ibid., 253.

[24] Morris, *The Apostolic Preaching of the Cross.*, 254.

[25] Murray, *Redemption Accomplished and Applied,* 126.

that this passage emphasizes justification as a legal "declaration." As Murray notes, "The meaning is simple ... the judges ... were to declare the righteous to be righteous, just as they were to declare the wicked to be wicked."[27]

The word's forensic nature can also be seen in Isa 5:23 ("Who justify the wicked for a bribe, And take away the rights of the ones who are right!") in which an unrighteous judge is seen declaring a righteous defendant to be unrighteous even though the defendant is inherently right.[28] Furthermore, Job (in chapter 13:18) expects a forensic declaration from God whom he has been seeking as a judge ("Behold now, I have prepared my case: I know that I will be vindicated"). This forensic understanding is strengthened in Ps 51:4 ("Against You, You only, I have sinned, and done what is evil in Your sight, so that You are justified when You speak, and blameless when You judge.") because to justify is applied to YHWH and "it is an impossible thought that He should be 'made righteous' in any sense other than 'made righteous before men'" by declaration.[29]

## The Greek term

Likewise, the δικαιόω word group has a forensic meaning. Specifically, the verbal form δικαιόω means "to declare righteous."[30] The Greek words used in the NT are δικαιοσύνη (*dikaiosunē*) and δικαιόω (*dikaioō*). *TDNT* tells us that δικαιόω is derived from δίκαιος (*dikaios*) and means "to establish as right," or, more importantly, "to validate."[31] The word group, according to W. E. Vine, expresses the

---

[26] Morris, *The Apostolic Preaching of the Cross,* 254.

[27] Murray, *Redemption Accomplished and Applied,* 126.

[28] Morris, *The Apostolic Preaching of the Cross*, 261.

[29] Morris, *The Apostolic Preaching of the Cross*, 260.

[30] *EDNTW,* "Justification", 2:284.

[31] *TDNT,* "δικαιόω," 2:211.

idea of "to pronounce or declare righteous."[32] The word group emphasizes a legal or a forensic perspective. *TDNT* makes a strong statement in this regard: "In the NT it is seldom that one cannot detect the legal connection."[33] Further, "In Paul the legal usage is plain and indisputable."[34]

*NIDNTTE* agrees with this assessment by stating "Undoubtedly, however, the legal and ethical aspects were of special importance. The adj. is common as a neut. noun in the sense of 'that which is [legally or ethically] right.'"[35] It is a legal or forensic term describing the action of a judge in a judicial setting. The judge renders a verdict after hearing the evidence against a defendant, who although being guilty of the charges brought against him, could still pronounce or declare the defendant not guilty and righteous. The consequence of the wrong action is removed by the legal or forensic pronouncement (declaration) of the judge even though the past wrong action cannot be erased. The defendant is *considered* innocent or guiltless of the wrong actions and his consequence for the wrong action is removed through the forensic (legal), monergistic pronouncement or declaration by the judge.

## Monergism

At this point it is important to define the term monergism. Monergism is a compound word composed of μόνος (*monos*), meaning "sole," and ἔργον (*ergon*), meaning "work," and results in the meaning "working alone" or "the sole worker." Theologically, MacArthur and Mayhue define monergism as "The view that regeneration is accomplished exclusively by the working of God."[36] Gregg R. Allison defines the word as the way to describe "that God

---

[32] *EDNTW*, "Justification," 2:284.

[33] *TDNT*, "δικαιόω," 2:214.

[34] Ibid., 2:215.

[35] *NIDNTTE*, "δικαιοσύνη," 1:723.

[36] MacArthur and Mayhue, *Biblical Doctrine*, 933.

alone saves human beings."[37] He points out that "justification exemplifies monergism" in Romans 4:5 to show that man contributes nothing for his salvation. In this verse, Paul is showing that God is the sole worker or single agent in man's salvation. In fact, as I am about to show, the Apostle Paul uses δικαιοσύνη and δικαιόω twenty-five times to describe the work of God *ALONE* in justification without exception.

## Synergism

In contrast to monergism, synergism is a salvific term that describes a cooperative effort between God and man.[38] Allison notes that some theologians use the term as God and human beings operating together to rescue man salvifically.[39] In fact, Ware describes the Eastern Orthodox understanding of salvation as "synergistic."[40]

## The Significance of Forensic Monergism

*NIDNTTE* calls this forensic, monergistic work "of special significance" by noting that Paul's statement in Romans 3:21–26 is prefaced by the statement, "therefore no one will be declared righteous [δικαιωθήσεται, *dikaiōthēsetai,* "will be justified"] in God's sight by the works of the law."[41] As Anthony N. S. Lane has well said, the instrument of justification is faith and is activated not by what it achieves but by what it receives.[42]

MacArthur and Mayhue emphasize the forensic or legal

---

[37] Gregg R. Allison, *The Baker Compact Dictionary of Theological Terms* (Grand Rapids: Baker, 2016), 139.

[38] MacArthur and Mayhue, *Biblical Doctrine*, 938.

[39] Allison, *The Baker Compact Dictionary of Theological Terms*, 205.

[40] Ware, *The Orthodox Church*, 221–22, 224.

[41] *NIDNTTE*, "δικαιοσύνη," 1:735.

[42] Anthony N. S. Lane, *Justification by Faith in Catholic-Protestant Dialogue: An Evangelical Assessment* (London: T&T Clark, 2002), 26.

meaning of justification's lexical nature when they define justification as the "Declaration that the person has been restored to a state of righteousness through belief and trust in the work of Christ rather than on the basis of one's own accomplishments."[43] Grudem emphasizes the immediate effect of justification when he defines justification as "An instantaneous legal act of God in which he (1) thinks of our sins as forgiven and Christ's righteousness as belonging to us, and (2) declares us to be righteous in his sight."[44] John Murray has well said, "In a word, justification is a declaration or pronouncement respecting the relation of the person to the law which he, the judge, is required to administer."[45] Brian Vickers also confirms that justification is "the legal declaration from God that a person stands before him forgiven and as one who lives up to the entirety of God's will."[46]

## THE SOURCE OF JUSTIFICATION:

### God's Declaration of Man's Efforts

But who is making the "declaration" in the redemption of man and why? The Greek text is very precise not only in the contextual study but also in the grammar. There are plenty of examples from which to find the answers to this question. The verbal form (δικαιόω) is used thirty-eight times in the New Testament. It is used ten times in the Gospels and Acts, three times by James and twenty-five times by Paul. To answer the question above we will begin with a quick summary of the word's use in the Gospels and Acts.

---

[43] MacArthur and Mayhue, *Biblical Doctrine*, 932. This restoration should be seen as the appearance before God as righteous rather than an actual or initial state of righteousness. This *declared righteousness* becomes *actual* when we see Jesus (1 John 3:2).

[44] Grudem, *Systematic Theology*, 1246.

[45] Murray, *Redemption Accomplished and Applied* (Grand Rapids: Eerdmans, 2015), 125.

[46] Brian Vickers, *Justification by Grace through Faith* (Phillipsburg, NJ: P&R, 2012), 2.

**Justification in the Gospels and Book of Acts**

There are two non-redemptive uses of δικαιόω in the Gospels where a man is described as justifying himself. In Luke 10:29, a lawyer justifies or declares his actions righteous before Jesus, and in Luke 16:15, Jesus condemns the Pharisees for justifying themselves as righteous before God.

Furthermore, Matt 11:19 and Luke 7:35 describe non-redemptive incidents where Jesus criticizes the Pharisees for their hypocritical evaluation of Him as well as John the Baptist by noting that His and John's testimonies will be justified (or vindicated) as righteous when truth about them is fully revealed. In Luke 7:29, after hearing Jesus exalt the work of John the Baptist, the tax collectors justified (or, acknowledged) God's work through John the Baptist. The tax collectors declared this to both the Pharisees and lawyers who were knowledgeable in Mosaic law because they had been baptized by John the Baptist.

## LUKE 18:9-14: An Important Prelude to Understanding Redemptive Justification

In Matthew 12 and Luke 18 we begin to see a direct connection between justification and redemption. In Matt 12:37, Jesus says to the Pharisees that they will be justified or condemned by what they say about Him. In Luke 18:14, Jesus tells us that a prerequisite for redemptive justification is humility. Luke 18:9–14 is an important text on justification. In the context, Jesus—according to Luke— uses a parable to show the folly of a self-righteous person who believes he is better than others in the sight of God (v9). In fact, Luke uses a word to describe the attitude of the self-righteous toward those around him that means to despise or to look upon with contempt. To show the danger of trusting one's self-righteous attitude for justification before God, Jesus contrasts the prayers of two men— a self-righteous Pharisee (v10–12) and a tax-collector (v10,13). The Pharisee justified himself before God by contrasting his righteousness with that of a tax-collector. To appreciate the teaching of Jesus and the contrast He is about to make, we need to understand who the Pharisees and tax-collectors were and how they were viewed in the

First century.

## Understanding the Pharisees

There were around six thousand Pharisees living in Israel at the time of Jesus' ministry.[47] They believed the Babylonian exile in the sixth century BC was divine punishment on their ancestors for breaking the Law of God rather than seeing the exile as the divine wrath on their ancestors for abandoning the singular worship of YHWH. Their solution for avoiding future divine punishment was seeking to be legally pure before YHWH. To be legally pure in their way of thinking was meticulous obedience to YHWH's law. In their way of thinking, God's law rather than God's grace was the way to divine justification.

## Understanding the Tax Collectors

In contrast to the Pharisees were the tax-collectors. In Jesus' day, the Jews as well as the rest of the Mediterranean world were under the control of the Roman Empire. As the ones in control, the Romans demanded tribute to be paid to them. Tribute was collected in the form of taxation upon the people. Rather than collect the taxes themselves, the Romans employed the local peoples to collect the taxes for them. In order to find the right people for tax-collection, the Romans sold the rights in an area to the highest bidder. The tax-collectors in Israel were Jews who purchased the right from the Roman government to collect the taxes and they were given the right to set the tax at their discretion as long as they collected the amount for the area set by Rome.[48] The tax-collectors were known for overcharging the people in their area and becoming personally wealthy at the expense of their countrymen. As a result, they were despised by the Jewish people and regarded as traitors because they worked to enrich themselves and the Romans at the expense of their fellow countrymen.

---

[47] Ralph Gower, *The New Manner and Customs of Bible Times* (Chicago: Moody Press, 1987), 256.
[48] Gower, 178

## Understanding the Contrasts in the Parables

In the parable, a Pharisee and a tax-collector enter the Temple to pray (v.10). The Pharisee praises his virtue before God and thanks God that he (the Pharisee) is not one of the "spiritually" and therefore legally impure like the swindler, the unjust, the adulterer or the tax-collector. That the tax-collector is listed last is no accident in the mind of the Pharisee. The tax-collector was considered the lowest of the low. Unlike these "low-life's," the Pharisee fasted twice per week rather than only at the religious festivals and faithfully paid his tithes—a sign of his strict adherence to the law of God.

On the other hand, the tax-collector in the parable is portrayed as a humble man before God. He refuses to enter the temple area, refuses to lift his eyes to heaven in addressing God and beats his breast while pleading for divine mercy (v.13). Rather than extolling his own merits and character like the Pharisee, *he appeals to God's mercy for justification.*

## The Lesson of the Parables

Jesus is quick to pronounce that the tax-collector was justified in God's sight rather than the Pharisee because of his (the tax-collector's) humility before God (v.14). While the Pharisee thought and attempted to offer his own righteousness to God for justification, Jesus instead condemned him for his arrogant assumption. On the other hand, Jesus declares the tax-collector justified in the sight of God because of his recognition that he had nothing to offer God on his (the tax-collector's) behalf. He came with only the desire for God's mercy and in the parable, he leaves justified. What a beautiful picture of divine justification.

## Gospel Conclusions

The uses of δικαιόω in Matthew and Luke describe men either justifying or declaring themselves righteous for their actions, or Jesus giving a general statement about what it means to be justified before God. The specifics of salvific justification in these references, however, are not yet stated with precision. The use of δικαιόω as a precise term to describe salvific justification will be developed by the Apostle Paul.

## A Clear Statement of Redemptive Justification in The Book of Acts

But finally, in Acts 13:38–39, there is a clear statement from Paul's preaching. It shows the contrast of a man's inability through the Law to accomplish justification for redemptive purposes and clearly states that justification is accomplished by faith alone in Christ's work. Although it is a general statement from Paul and the only time justification by faith is mentioned in the Book of Acts,[49] he is making an important statement on justification through faith alone in contrast to works. It is a distinction Paul will develop in greater detail within his correspondence to the Galatian churches not long after making this statement, and later in a letter to the Christians of Rome that he will compose a few years later.[50] Luther thought so highly of these two verses that he wrote in the *Preface to the Acts of the Apostles* (1533), "It should be noted that by this book St Luke teaches the whole of Christendom ... that the true and chief article of Christian doctrine is this: We must all be justified alone by faith in Jesus Christ, without any contribution from the law or help from our works. This doctrine is the chief intention of the book and the author's principal reason for writing it."[51] As Luther notes, this passage deserves greater consideration.

Acts 13:38–39 comes at the climax of Paul's sermon in Pisidian Antioch. It is Paul's concluding remarks to his Jewish audience calling for a decision involving spiritual life or death.[52] He is speaking to those who love the Mosaic Law and who base their hope of blessing from God on their obedience to the Law.[53] Paul's

---

[49] Francis Martin, *Acts*, ACCS, (Downers Grove, IL: InterVarsity, 2006), 168.

[50] John R. W. Stott, *The Message of Acts*, BST (Downers Grove, IL: InterVarsity, 1994), 225.

[51] Stott., 226.

[52] Ibid., 225.

[53] James Montgomery Boice, *Acts* (Grand Rapids: Baker, 1997), 240.

argument is that Mosaic Law provides no hope for justification and could never provide justification. Instead, as F. F. Bruce states, "believers in Christ are completely justified .... In other words, Moses' law does not justify; faith in Christ does."[54] Paul closes his sermon in verses 40–41, imploring those in Pisidian Antioch to heed the message of the Prophets by quoting specifically from Hab 1:5 ("Behold, you scoffers, and marvel, and perish, for I am accomplishing a work in your days, a work which you will never believe, though someone should describe it to you."). It was an effective message because verses 42–43 report that the audience was begging for more, and many Jews and God-fearing proselytes began following the teaching of Paul and Barnabus.

**A Challenge From The Book of James**

James, however, gives us a potentially different usage of the word δικαιόω. In Jas 2:21–26, he contrasts living faith with dead faith.[55] In Jas 2:21 and 24, he makes plain that Abraham was justified by works and not by faith.[56] He follows this up in verse 25 with another clear statement that Rahab was also justified by works.[57] Is

---

[54] F. F. Bruce, *The Book of the Acts*, NICNT (Grand Rapids: Eerdmans, 1976), 278–279.

[55] John MacArthur, *James,* MacNTC (Chicago: Moody, 1998), 135.

[56] *EDNTW*, 2:286. Vine makes a helpful observation on the difference between Paul's and James' use of justification. He notes that Paul in Gal 3:6 is quoting from Gen 15:6, where God establishes His covenant with Abram as he moves from Ur to the Promised Land, while James is basing his argument on Gen 22:18, where God intervenes at the sacrifice of Isaac. The significance is that Paul is referencing Abraham's initial faith that results in justification while James is referencing the vindication of Abraham's faith as he acts to conduct God's difficult request to sacrifice Isaac. As Vine rightly notes, Paul is using Gen 15:6 to emphasize justification's relational element while James' use of Gen 22:18 emphasizes the conduct of one who is justified.

[57] MacArthur, Hebrews, *MacNTC* (Nashville: Thomas Nelson, 2007), 799. MacArthur insightfully notes that Rahab had already expressed her faith or confidence in YHWH, now she is demonstrating her faith by hiding the spies. He goes on to rightly note that Heb 11:31 declares that the faith of Rahab—not her works—saved her.

James teaching that works find favor with God for salvation?

A careful examination of the text will show that James is not speaking of the initial expression of faith that results in "being declared righteous" for redemptive purposes. Instead, James describes a previously expressed faith that is manifested by works. Donald Guthrie notes that James in his well-known passage of James 2:14-26 "is not decrying the need for faith, for he assumes this is a basis."[58]

The writers of the *Open Bible* present an instructive outline for understanding the letter of James.[59] They divide the book into three parts: chapter 1:1–18 ("The Test of Faith"); chapters 1:19–5:6 ("The Characteristics of Faith"), and chapter 5:7–20 ("The Triumph of Faith"). Why would they describe the organization of the Letter of James around the idea of faith when Chapter 2:14–26 clearly states that works—in contrast to faith—justify?

A careful reading of Jas 2:14–26 will show that James is not highlighting works at the expense of faith. A. T. Robertson calls this "the famous passage that is supposed by some scholars to be an attack on Paul's doctrine of salvation by faith."[60] It should be noted that the discussion begins in Jas 2:14 with an evaluation of genuine faith: "… if a man says he has faith …" As MacArthur comments, "The genuineness of a profession of Jesus Christ as Savior and Lord is evidenced more by what a person does than by what he claims."[61] Hiebert notes James is saying "that an inoperative faith is useless."[62] Robertson summarizes James' thoughts by saying that he "looks upon works as a proof of faith, not as means of salvation."[63]

---

[58] Donald Guthrie, *New Testament Introduction* (Downers Grove, IL: InterVarsity, 1968), 768.

[59] *The Open Bible*, expanded, (Nashville: Thomas Nelson, 1985), 1253.

[60] A. T. Robertson, *Studies in the Epistle of James* (Nashville: Broadman Press, 1959), 91.

[61] MacArthur, *James, 199.*

[62] D. Edmond Hiebert, *The Epistles of James* (Chicago: Moody Press, 1979), 175.

James then goes on to evaluate faith by the works it produces. More importantly, James in 2:18 contrasts the one who says he has faith but no works to verify his profession with the one who says others can verify his profession by his works. James is proclaiming that a person's works serve to verify his profession of faith.[64] He is not contradicting Paul; he is demonstrating that genuine faith will demonstrate itself with appropriate action. Paul will write later, in Galatians and Romans, to clarify the difference in relationship between salvific faith and its demonstration through works. James is not saying—in the context of his writing—that works save. He is saying that faith will be demonstrated in the life of the one professing it through his actions (works).

Daniel Doriani insightfully describes James' statement by saying, "Real faith does express itself in acts of love."[65] If the biblical canon did not include Romans and Galatians for support in addition to a careful contextual understanding of James statements, one could be inclined to accept James' assertions that works justify. While Paul demonstrates that faith justifies, James reminds Jesus' disciples that works only confirm justification or demonstrate one's profession of faith.

**Paul's Support of Divine Monergistic Justification**

It was mentioned earlier that Paul in Acts 13:38–39 contrasts the inability of the Law to work justification in a person for salvation while faith in Christ's work certainly does. The table in Appendix One shows Paul's other 25 uses of the word δικαιόω.

The argument being made by Paul under the inspiration of the Holy Spirit is that δικαιόω is a forensic, monergistic, declaration by God conferred through faith on the redeemed of God.[66] How does the grammar support the lexical concept of divine, forensic, monergistic

---

[63] Robertson, *Studies in the Epistle of James*, 92.

[64] MacArthur, *James*, 129.

[65] Daniel M. Doriani, *James*, REC (Philipsburg, NJ: P&R Publishing, 2007), 88.

[66] See the definition of "Justification" in the Introduction.

justification in Pauline writings?

While the answer to this question is strongly affirmed with Paul's use of the passive voice, Paul's five uses or twenty percent of his use of δικαιόω are in the active voice and must also be considered (in the active voice the subject does the action of the verb). In all five instances where δικαιόω is used in the active voice (Rom 3:30; 4:5; 8:30; 8:33; and Gal 3:8), God is the one that is justifying. Therefore, Paul is stating that justification is the result of a monergistic, divine act!

Paul uses the remainder of the references (20 verbal forms, of which 4 are participles and 2 are infinitives) in the passive voice. His purpose is to emphasize who is performing the work of justification. Does Paul's use of the passive in the work of justification demonstrate justification to be a divinely, monergistic work or does it show a divine and human, synergistic work? Does grammar really assist us in answering this question?

The passive voice is used to describe that the subject is receiving the action of the verb. David Alan Black explains: "In the passive voice the subject is pictured as being acted upon."[67] In 80% of Paul's usage of δικαιόω, all the ones being acted upon or being "declared righteous" (justified) are receiving the divine declaration (justification) monergistically through faith alone. Those who are being divinely acted upon are repentant sinners who have embraced with confidence Jesus' work on the cross and have become one of His followers. Paul reenforces this monergistic point using the active voice in Rom 8:30 and 8:33 but makes the point by using the passive in Rom 4:2, 5; 5:1, 9; 6:7; Gal 2:16, 17; 3:8, 11, 24; 5:4; and Titus 3:7.

Paul's use of δικαιόω indicates that justification is a forensic declaration by God conferred upon the redeemed through faith alone. The lexical meaning of δικαιόω is embedded with this forensic thought.[68] The divine, monergistic work of this declaration, then, is

---

[67] David Alan Black, *Learn To Read New Testament Greek* (Nashville: B&H, 2009), 13.

[68] Morris, *The Apostolic Preaching of the Cross*, 283.

clearly stated grammatically and it is made forcefully by Paul using the passive voice, and reenforced by his use of the active. The lexical and grammatical use of δικαιόω by Paul—the primary user of δικαιόω in the New Testament—shows 100% of the time that δικαιόω is a divine, forensic, monergistic work.

So how did the Roman Catholic and the Eastern Orthodox Churches undo the lexical and grammatical understanding of δικαιόω, and why have some Protestant groups adopted Eastern Orthodox thinking in the form of Arminianism? This will be the task for the remainder of this book.

# CHAPTER FOUR
# THE ROLE UNDERSTANDING IMPUTATION PLAYS IN DEFINING JUSTIFICATION

## Imputation

Closely related to the biblical understanding of justification is the understanding of imputation. The Greek word translated "imputation," λογίζομαι (*logizomai*), is used forty times in the New Testament, with thirty-four occurrences in the Pauline writings. In Romans, Paul uses λογίζομαι nineteen times and another eight in 1 Corinthians, which is important to note in the quest to understand the forensic nature of justification.

The term λογίζομαι in the Greek world was used both in accounting and general contexts.[69] Plato used the word philosophically to mean "to grasp and apply facts."[70] *TDNT* says it was used philosophically to mean "to deliberate or conclude."[71]

But λογίζομαι was most commonly used in the financial and commercial world.[72] In this context λογίζομαι means "to calculate, to reckon"[73] in reference to record keeping or "to credit something to someone that comes from another."[74] It is this sense of reckoning or consideration that biblical scholars understand the term.[75] Therefore, Grudem can rightly say that to impute means "To think of as belonging to someone, and therefore to cause it to belong to that

---

[69] *NIDNTTE*, "λογίζομαι," 3:123.

[70] Silva., 3:124.

[71] *TDNT*, "λογίζομαι," 4:284.

[72] Ibid., 4:284; see also Tremper Longman III, "Impute, Imputation," *The Baker Compact Bible Dictionary* (Grand Rapids: Baker, 2014), 170.

[73] *NIDNTTE*, "λογίζομαι," 3:123.

[74] Longman III, "Impute, Imputation," 170.

[75] MacArthur and Mayhue, *Biblical Doctrine*, 618.

person."[76]

The koine Greek definition and the etymological development of λογίζομαι (imputation) shows that it is used in both a limited, general, philosophical sense but most commonly as a mathematical term used in finances and commerce. The word expresses *an objective consideration* rather than a *subjective infusion*. In Christian theological understanding, whether it refers to an *objective consideration* or a *subjective infusion* is the crux of the issue.

Philosophically from the koine perspective, λογίζομαι (imputation) is *an objective consideration or an evaluation based on facts* that results in a *declared* conclusion. Commercially, the *objective concept* imbedded in the understanding of λογίζομαι (imputation) also remains in the understanding of the word. It is a ledger entry that is considered before being applied to an individual's account with the result that it makes the recipient accountable for what was entered. Therefore, to say that Christ's righteousness has been imputed to the one embracing confidence in Jesus' work on the cross (Romans 3 and 4) is to say that Christ's righteousness is considered by God, who is the Supreme accountant, to be applied to the account of the one embracing confidence in Jesus' work on the cross. MacArthur and Mayhue correctly emphasize this concept of λογίζομαι in their definition of the imputation of Christ's righteousness when they define it as "God's act of crediting the righteousness of Christ to sinners who trust him for salvation."[77] As a result, whether it is used philosophically or commercially, λογίζομαι (imputation) is the objective way for someone other than yourself to view your reality in contrast to your taking on a reality you desire to receive that is outside yourself."

Why is it so important to understand the difference between an objective "reckoned or considered" imputed righteousness in contrast to a subjective "infused" imputed righteousness? To answer this question, we must understand what it

---

[76] Grudem, *Systematic Theology*, 1245.

[77] John MacArthur and Richard Mayhue, *Biblical Doctrine: A Systematic Summary of Bible Truth*, 931.

means to be infused and how an objective consideration is different from a subjective infusion. Synonyms for the word infusion would include injection, insertion, or implantation. The word injection is especially useful here for illustrative purposes because the idea of going to the doctor to receive a shot or an injection to fight infection illustrates the thought that is <u>*NOT*</u> intended by Paul's use of λογίζομαι.

Many Christians erroneously think of justification as an infusion, an injection, an insertion, or an implantation of righteousness from God. They see the reception of the shot as their subjective experience in justification—meaning that they believe actual righteousness is being infused, injected, or implanted into the redeemed. If this is true (and linguistically it is not), then philosophically we have a problem. What happens to righteousness when a redeemed person sins?

Some theologians solve this dilemma by suggesting that salvation has been lost but can be regained by another "infusion" of the re-birth experience (similar in the current COVID circumstances to being re-vaccinated)! But this understanding is not only against the teaching from God's Word (Romans 8:31-39; John 10:27-29 to name a few instances which teach that salvation cannot be lost) it also ignores the meaning of the Greek word λογίζομαι (imputation) which does not contain the concept of infusion. Nor does this convey the divine concept Paul is inspired to write when he uses the word.

The proper way of understanding λογίζομαι is reinforced by Paul's use of δικαιόω (justification) as an objective, forensic or legal statement by a judge pronouncing a legal decision. His pronouncement or declaration does not change the present subjective nature of the accused. Rather, the declared decision only changes the present objective position of the sinner before our holy God. This results in making the declaration a present objective acceptance by God but not yet a subjective reality.

But λογίζομαι (imputation) also reinforces this objective idea proclaimed by δικαιόω (to declare righteous). So, whether you begin by trying to understand λογίζομαι, or by trying to understand δικαιόω, they are both objective terms used to describe a present objective reality – acceptance by God in the present time with a promise of a complete subjective reality when we see Jesus face-to-face (1 John 3:2).

Λογίζομαι (imputation) is not a subjective term (meaning to inject, to insert, to implant) but an objective term (meaning to consider, to reckon, to regard). Λογίζομαι does not take on a subjective understanding based on a theologian's philosophical desire. It is an objective term used by Paul to carry the concept or idea of *"to consider as having the quality of something without actually having its possession."* Our full possession of Christ's righteousness does not occur in the redeemed until we see Jesus (1 John 3:2). Until then, the redeemed sinner appears or looks righteous in God's eyes because the Father sees us through the shed blood of Jesus which acts as a lens on the figurative eyeglasses of God while He perseveres in us for our glorification.

J. D. Douglas and Merrill C. Tenney show a helpful progression in the discussion of imputed justification. They note that Paul in Rom 5:12–21 argues Adam's sin was imputed by God to all humankind. Then, Paul argues in 2 Cor 5:19, 21 that God imputes mankind's sin to Christ. And finally, in Rom 3–4 God imputes Christ's righteousness to believers.[78]

Is there a biblical example of righteousness being imputed to a believer in the manner described above? This is where the Hebrew Scriptures provide helpful examples. Leviticus 7:18 and 17:4 describe imputation in the same way it is used in the New Testament. In fact, the LXX uses the word λογίζομαι to translate the Hebrew word חָשַׁב (*chashab*). Intriguingly, like λογίζομαι, the Hebrew word contains the philosophical understanding of imputation.[79]

What is being imputed in Lev 7:18 and 17:4? Leviticus 7:18 focuses on the peace offering. The peace offering is first introduced in Lev 3 where general instructions are given for the sacrifice. George

---

[78] J. D. Douglas and Merrill C. Tenney, *The New International Dictionary of the Bible* (Grand Rapids: Zondervan, 1987), 464.

[79] *BDB*, "חָשַׁב," 363.

Bush identifies Lev 7:11–18 with the heading "Additional Rules respecting the Peace offerings."[80] According to 7:12 and 16, there are two types of peace offerings. The first type of peace offering mentioned in verse 12 is done as a token of appreciation to Yahweh for special favors and mercies received from Him.[81] The second type mentioned in verse 16 is a votive or freewill offering that was to be offered at the completion of a vow.[82]

According to verse 15, the peace offering presented to Yahweh as a token of appreciation for special favors and mercies received from Him *must* be eaten on the day of the sacrifice; there were to be no leftovers. By contrast, in verse 16 a votive or freewill offering *should* be eaten on the day it was sacrificed, and any leftovers could be eaten the following day. However, if leftovers remained on the third day following the sacrifice, they must be burned by fire and not eaten. Leviticus 7:18 states there is a consequence for eating rather than burning the leftovers on the third day—the offering will be rejected by Yahweh and the benefits will no longer be *imputed* (reckoned or considered) to the offeree.

In Lev 17:4, Moses tells the Israelites that the improper killing of an animal, in this case because of the sacrifice's location, is considered by God to be blood guiltiness. In other words, improperly killing an animal is like killing a human being and brings imputed guilt upon the sacrifice—the sacrifice will not be accepted by God and the one sacrificing will be considered guilty of bloodshed in God's eyes.[83]

It is clear, therefore, by both the lexical meaning and contextual intention, that λογίζομαι is to be understood in an objective rather than subjective sense. Imputation is a conferred consideration

---

[80] George Bush, *Notes on Leviticus* (Minneapolis: James & Klock, 1976), 68.

[81] Ibid., 68.

[82] Bush, *Notes on Leviticus.*, 69.

[83] Ibid., 166–167.

rather than a conferred infusion upon the recipient. More importantly, this understanding of imputation complements the forensic nature of λογίζομαι. The court has no power to infuse its decision upon the defendant to change his or her nature, but it can impart a declaration that causes the recipient to be viewed by all observers in a different manner. As MacArthur and Mayhue say, imputation is the "judicial reckoning or forensic transfer of one's person's sin or righteousness to another."[84] Grudem simplifies the understanding of imputation even more by saying, "When we say that God *imputes* Christ's righteousness to us it means that God *thinks* of Christ's righteousness as belonging to us or regards it *as belonging to* us."[85]

The lexical understanding of imputation is contrary to the thinking on imputation in Eastern Orthodoxy, Roman Catholicism and Arminianism. All three of these "expressions" of Christianity conceive of Christ's righteousness as infusion into a believer at justification. Thus, they are redefining the biblical term imputation (λογίζομαι) which has the meaning of "to calculate or reckon." In place of the lexical meaning and concept of the Greek word, they impose the idea of "infusion" which is a foreign understanding of this term. The lesson that we learn is that when one deviates from the meaning of a word in Scripture and imposes a foreign understanding in the place of its lexical meaning, it alters the concept God was conveying in His inspired Word. In this case, the redefinition of justification and imputation produces a false gospel that stands under the anathema of Galatians 1:6-9.

---

[84] MacArthur and Mayhue, *Biblical Doctrine*, 931.

[85] Grudem, *Systematic Theology*, 726; emphasis original.

# CHAPTER FIVE

# THE HISTORICAL RE-DEFINITION OF JUSTIFICATION

## The Root of Definitional Change

In the early centuries of Christianity, there should have been little difficulty in understanding and defining δικαιοσύνη, δίκαίωσις, and δικαιόω in a forensic, divine, monergistic sense. We have recovered 5,735 extant Greek manuscripts. All of these copies of the originals can be dated between the 2nd and 15th centuries[86] with many of them being dated within the first four centuries of the originals.[87]

Additionally, we have numerous writings from the Patristic Fathers that are preserved in the Greek language.[88] One would think that it would be safe, then, to conclude that the Patristic Fathers (using the Greek texts) understood the meaning of δικαιοσύνη, and δικαιόω to be a "declared righteousness" from the judicial sense as defined in Chapter Two. Clement of Rome, who lived in the first century, wrote, "Having been called through his [God's] will in Christ Jesus, [we] are not justified through ourselves or through our own wisdom or understanding or piety or works which we have done in holiness of heart, but through faith by which the Almighty God has justified all who have existed from the beginning."[89] This understanding of justification, however, did not continue to be embraced by the church after the time of Constantine. The change in thinking can initially be traced to whether a particular Patristic Father was located in either the Eastern or Western Church.

What was the difference between the Eastern and Western Patristic Fathers that influenced their understanding of δικαιοσύνη

---

[86] Josh McDowell, *The New Evidence That Demands A Verdict* (Nashville: Thomas Nelson, 1999), 34.

[87] McDowell, Josh., 36.

[88] F. F. Bruce, *The New Testament Documents*, 6th ed. (Grand Rapids: Eerdmans, 1981), 14.

[89] Cited in Gregg R. Allison, *Historical Theology: An Introduction to Christian Doctrine* (Grand Rapids: Zondervan, 2011), 499.

and δικαιόω? While Greek continued to be the universal language of the Mediterranean world as it had been since the time of Alexander the Great, there was a competing "universal" language vying for dominance. With the defeat of Greece by the Romans in 31 BC,[90] the Latin language became a competing force.

Until the mid-third century AD, Greek was the preferred language within the Church.[91] But by the end of the 2nd century, Latin translations of the Bible were beginning to be used in North Africa, and Tertullian was introducing Christianized Latin into the Church.[92] Although Clement of Rome wrote his *Epistle to the Corinthians* in Greek, it was translated into Latin.[93] By the 4th century, the Western Fathers were writing primarily in Latin while the Eastern Fathers continued using Greek. Making Latin the ecclesiastical language in the West had an impact on the difference in the theological thinking of the Eastern and Western Churches, especially in their understanding of justification.

### Justification to Chrysostom and Ambrosiaster

The Eastern Church Father John Chrysostom (349–407) communicated an understanding of justification *by faith alone*. He wrote, "The patriarch Abraham himself before receiving circumcision had been declared righteous on the score of faith alone."[94] Commenting on Rom 4:1, he said, "For a person who had no works, to be justified by faith, was nothing unlikely. But for a person richly adorned with good deeds, not to be made just from hence, but from

---

[90] Arnold J. Toynbee, *A Study of History* (New York & London: Oxford University Press, 1961), 561.

[91] Christine Mohrmann, "How Latin Came to Be the Language of Early Christendom," *Irish Quarterly Journal Review 40,* no. 159 (Sept 1951): 277–88.

[92] Mohrmann, 283.

[93] Mohrmann.

[94] Philip Schaff, *St. Chrysostom: Homilies on Acts and Romans*, vol. 11, NPNF (Peabody, MA: Hendrickson Publishers, 1995), 385.

faith, this was the thing to cause wonder, and to set the power of faith in a strong light."[95] In his Homily on Eph 4:2 and 9 he wrote; "No one, Paul says, is justified by works, precisely in order that grace and benevolence may become apparent."[96]

Chrysostom's writings express his view that the justification of man is divinely monergistic. It is not accomplished by the action of man but solely by the action of God. Although Chrysostom does not identify with precision the forensic nature of justification, he notes that a man's confidence is to be in God for justification—not in man's action, work, or effort. The forensic nature of δικαιοσύνη, and δικαιόω appear to be implied in Chrysostom's understanding of the word group. This is likely due to the natural, inherent understanding of the Greek word negating the need to highlight this aspect of justification.

Ambrosiaster, named so by Erasmus as the author whose works were once attributed to Ambrose, was active on the other side of the empire in Rome and a contemporary of Chrysostom and Augustine.[97] He also left the church strong, biblical statements on justification by faith alone. In remarks written between 366–384 AD regarding Rom 3:24, he said, "They are justified freely because they have not done anything nor given anything in return, but only by faith alone they have been made holy by the gift of God."[98] Commenting on Rom 4:5, he says,

> How then can the Jews think that they have been justified by the works of the law in the same way as Abraham, when they see that Abraham was not justified by the works of the law but by faith alone? Therefore, there is no need of the law when the

---

[95] Schaff., 385.

[96] Mark Edwards, *Galatians, Ephesians, Philippians*, ACCS (Downers Grove, IL: InterVarsity Press, 1998), 6:110.

[97] Martin, *Acts*, 325.

[98] Gerald L. Bray, *Commentaries on Romans and 1-2 Corinthians*, ACT (Downers Grove, IL: InterVarsity, 2009), 29.

ungodly is justified before God by faith alone.[99]

In comments on Rom 4:6, he makes the simple statement, "They are justified before God by faith alone."[100] A plain reading of these writings demonstrate his belief that justification originates outside of man and is secured only by faith! This is another example of the early Church demonstrating a forensic understanding of the Greek word.

### Justification to Augustine and Cyril of Alexandria

Arguably the two most influential Patristic Fathers who shaped the minds of Western Church thinkers on justification from the 5th-century Church Fathers to the time of the Reformation were Augustine (354–430) and Cyril of Alexandria (376–444). In the 6th century, Germanic monks were engaged in a controversy with the Eastern Church whose capital was Constantinople[101] over Nestorianism[102] and Pelagianism.[103] They supported their position—

---

[99] Bray., 32.

[100] Bray.
[101] David R Maxwell, "Justification in the Early Church," *CJ* 44, no. 3 (2018): 25–40.

[102] MacArthur and Mayhue, *Biblical Doctrine*, 933. Nestorianism is the belief that Jesus Christ is two persons (a Divine and a Human) in one body. It was introduced by Nestorius (ca. 381–ca. 451) who rightly insisted that Mary did not give birth to Jesus' divine nature. Many, including Luther, claimed that Nestorius was misunderstood implying that his terminology was the source of the problem. Nevertheless, Nestorius is attributed with heresy and the definitive statement from the Council of Ephesus in 431 AD proclaiming that Jesus is one person with two natures remains the proper, biblically orthodox perspective of Jesus rather than two persons, two natures as Nestorius' terminology stated.

[103] John MacArthur and Richard Mayhue., 462, 934. Pelagius (ca. 354–ca.420) rejected the inherent sinfulness of man (total depravity) and taught that man is condemned by God only for his own personal sin. He concluded this without carefully considering Ephesians 2:1–10 that teaches the inability of man for self-transformation and Isaiah 64:6 which clearly states that man's efforts of righteousness are nothing more than filthy rags in the sight of God. Pelagius believed that man, through his own effort, could live a sinless life without divine grace.

which was in opposition to both the Pope in Rome and the Patriarch in Constantinople—by using Augustine's soteriology and Cyril's Christology to reject the insertion of merit into the Church's understanding of Christology and soteriology. Although the German monks (quoting Augustine and Cyril) did not assert that justification was a "declaration of righteousness" from God, they made it clear that a forensic, monergistic understanding of justification is inherent in their argument. This enforced the idea that merit before God comes from outside of man through faith alone.

T. F. Torrance suggested that no one in the early centuries of Christianity articulated the doctrine of justification by grace better than Cyril.[104] Augustine and Cyril were the two most quoted Patristic Fathers in the Book of Concord (1580).[105] But did Augustine and Cyril define justification in the same way? History shows that they did not. David Maxwell places the difference in their understanding of justification on language.[106] Busenitz would agree with this assessment of Augustine. He notes that Augustine's teaching on justification was inconsistent because he relied "on the Latin translation of the Bible, which caused him to miss, at times, the clear meaning of the original Greek and Hebrew terms for justification."[107]

Both Augustine and Cyril were conversant in the Greek language. However, while Cyril (a member of the Eastern Church) wrote in the Greek language, Augustine (a member of the Western Church) wrote in Latin. As a result, Augustine's Greek skills were not the same as Cyril's. Augustine admitted that his Greek skills were poor. In his *Confessions* (1.13-14), he admits the difficulty he had in his youth learning the Greek language and his regret at not learning it better when he wrote,

---

[104] Matthew Baker and Todd Speidell, *T. F. Torrance and Eastern Orthodoxy* (Eugene, OR: Wipf & Stock, 2015), 123.

[105] Maxwell, "Justification in the Early Church," 28.

[106] Ibid., 29–30.

[107] Nathan Busenitz, *Long Before Luther: tracing the heart of the Gospel from Christ to the Reformation* (Chicago: Moody Publishers, 2017), 127.

I sinned, then, when as a boy I preferred those empty to those more profitable studies .... Why then did I hate the Greek classics .... Difficulty, in truth, the difficulty of a foreign tongue .... For not one word of it did I understand, and to make me understand I was urged vehemently with cruel threats and punishments.[108]

The impact that communicating in Latin versus communicating in Greek had on the Church's understanding of justification will be developed more fully in a discussion on Jerome later in this book. But the "seeds" of difference between the Eastern and Western Church's understanding of justification were planted in the 4th century. The Eastern and Western churches were beginning to think differently because they used different ecclesiastical languages. Although some say that Augustine's Greek skills were poor because it was a second language to him, at least one linguist has concluded that his skills were comparable to any pastor today.[109] It is reasonable to conclude this to be true for the other Western Patristic Fathers.

While the Patristic Fathers did not always clearly define δικαιοσύνη and δικαιόω in the extant writings of their preaching, Augustine and Cyril did leave clear statements about justification by faith alone. Augustine wrote, "For of this it is written, 'Abraham believed God, and it was counted unto him for righteousness." And again, 'To him that believeth on Him that justifieth the ungodly, his faith is counted for righteousness."[110] This provides additional evidence of the monergistic understanding of justification in Augustine's thinking.

But did Augustine have a forensic concept of justification or was it a sanative one? Augustine is somewhat confusing to those who

---

[108] Todd Scacewater, "How Bad Were Augustine's Greek Skills?" exegeticaltools.com, *How Bad Were Augustine's Greek Skills?* (blog), August 13, 2017.

[109] Scacewater, "How Bad Were Augustine's Greek Skills?"

[110] Philip Schaff, *NPNF*, 14 vols. (Peabody, MA: Hendrickson Publishers, 1995), 5:107.

later read his writings. In the Western Church, both Roman Catholic and Protestant theologians claim Augustinian support of their theological thinking. While Augustine espoused the view that man could not come to saving faith under his own intellectual power and that saving faith is a result of divine action, his own definition of justification was a sanative, infused understanding, which he described as "to be made righteous by God" rather than the forensic understanding of "to be declared righteous by God."[111] This is corroborated by Robert Letham, who noted that Augustine used the Latin understanding of *iustificare* in defining justification as "to make righteous" in Rom 2:13.[112] Nathan Busenitz, in an excellent resource tracing the early church's understanding of justification, also notes that Augustine defined justification as "to make righteous."[113] Busenitz lists the primary reason for Augustine's definition as his reliance on the Latin translations of the Bible rather than the original languages of Scripture.[114] Furthermore, "Due to his reliance on the Latin text, he was blinded to the forensic meaning of the Greek—and the Hebrew—terms for justification in Scripture."[115]

Augustine would go on to say that "to be made righteous" by God was inherent in the grace He extended to man, and this shaped his understanding that aligned justification with sanctification. Busenitz notes that Augustine did not attempt to differentiate between justification and sanctification.[116] This blurring between justification and sanctification seemed to be prevalent at the time as we shall see in writings by Cyril of Alexandria. This blending of justification and sanctification was developed in the Eastern churches as *theosis*.[117]

---

[111] Ibid., 5:102.

[112] Letham, *Systematic Theology*, 679.

[113] Busenitz, *Long Before Luther*, 113.

[114] Busenitz., 113.

[115] Busenitz. See also 116.

[116] Busenitz., 112.

Augustine's definition is partially the result of challenging Pelagius' perspective of a man-centered salvation (based upon Pelagius' interpretation of Rom 2:13, "for not the hearers of the Law are just before God, but the doers of the Law will be justified"). Augustine was attempting to emphasize the Bible's God-centered perspective with his comment. However, his statement is more properly attributed to his reasoning in Latin rather than Greek.

Moreover, it should be noted that although Augustine had a conceptual understanding of "being made righteous" for δικαιόω, he also recognizes that being considered righteous by God is divinely initiated and accomplished by God rather than by man and is received by man only through faith. Therefore, as Busenitz notes, there are places where Augustine articulates a forensic sense of justification.[118] He cites Augustine's explanation of Ps 31 as an example where Augustine reflects on Rom 4:5 by saying,

> "When someone believes in him who justifies the impious, that faith is reckoned as justice to the believer, as David too declares that person blessed whom God has accepted and endowed with righteousness, independently of any righteous actions. What righteousness is this? The righteousness of faith, preceded by no good works, but with good works as its consequence."[119]

---

[117] Letham, *Systematic Theology*, 679. James Buchanan (*The Doctrine of Justification* [Grand Rapids: Baker Academic, 1997], 91) believed Augustine saw the distinction between justification and sanctification but Letham disagrees and the historical evidence appears to be weighted in Letham's favor. Alister E. McGrath ("Forerunners of the Reformation? A Critical Examination of the Evidence for Precursors of the Reformation Doctrines of Justification," *HTR* 75, no. 2 [April 1982]: 220) has a more extreme statement regarding Augustine's understanding of justification. He says, "It is utterly alien to Augustine's thought to speak of a forensic doctrine of justification; or of imputed righteousness in the Reformed sense of the term." While it is true that it appears Augustine did not have a completely "reformed" understanding of justification and its imputation, the quotes above indicate it was not entirely alien to his thinking.

[118] Busenitz, *Long Before Luther*, 118–119.

In a different place, Busenitz agrees with David F. Wright's assessment that Augustine described justification as a past event rather than an ongoing process in a believer's life.[120] Busenitz cites an example from Augustine's writings on Rom 8:30: "You are among the predestined, the called, the justified.... If the faith which works through love is in you, you already belong to the predestined, the called, the justified.... We are sons of God, predestined, called, justified; we are sons of God and what we shall be has not yet been revealed."[121] John Gerstner notes that while Augustine found justification and sanctification in association with each other, this does not mean they should not be distinguished from each other.[122] While many find Augustine's understanding of justification confusing and lacking a clear, forensic statement, he nonetheless associates a monergistic, initial divine action with the term.

Cyril, who was identified by Torrance as the most articulate early Church Father on justification, never used the exact phrase "justification by grace."[123] Cyril, like Augustine, was an African, although they lived in distinct parts of the Roman Empire and represented different church cultures. Augustine was a part of the Western Church; Cyril was integrated into the Eastern Church.

---

[119] Busenitz., 118. Busenitz quotes from Augustine's *Enarrat. Ps.,* 31.7. *PL* 36.263. Trans. From John E. Rotelle, *Expositions of the Psalms* 1-32 (Hyde Park, NY: New York City Press, 2000), 11:370.

[120] Ibid., 120.

[121] Ibid., 121.

[122] Ibid.

[123] Baker and Speidell, *T. F. Torrance and Eastern Orthodoxy*, 125. This assessment is made by Daniel Fairbairn in Chapter 6 of this book edited by Baker and Speidell. He, as well as the other contributors, are sympathetic to Torrance's endeavor to bring together Reformed and Eastern Orthodox theologians. While I do not agree that Reformed and Eastern Orthodox thinking are compatible on justification, sanctification, salvation, faith and grace, their evaluation of Cyril's thinking is helpful to understanding the confusion that has developed from those calling themselves the true church with a sanative understanding of justification in contrast to those with a forensic understanding of justification.

Augustine wrote and thought in Latin; Cyril wrote and thought in Greek.[124] While Augustine's doctrine of justification must be inferred from his writings, Cyril provided a definite doctrine of justification.

Cyril has some rich statements on justification. He said, For truly the compassion from beside the Father is Christ, as he takes away the sins, dismisses the charges and justifies by faith, and recovers the lost and makes [them] stronger than death.... For by him and in him we have known the Father, and we have become rich in the justification by faith.[125]

In addition, he said, "We are justified by faith, not by works of the Law, as Scripture says. By faith in whom, then, are we justified? Is it not in him who suffered death according to the flesh for our sake? Is it not in one Lord Jesus Christ? Have we not been redeemed by proclaiming his death and confessing his resurrection?"[126] Furthermore he wrote, "For truly the compassion from beside the Father is Christ, as he takes away the sins, dismisses the charges and justifies by faith, and recovers the lost and makes [them] stronger than death.... For by him and in him we have known the Father, and we have become rich in the justification by faith."[127]

Cyril is intriguing because he was one of the foundational shapers of deification (θέωσις) in the Eastern churches, using δικαιοσύνη and ἁγιασμός as virtual synonyms.[128] This resulted in a confusion within the Eastern Church between justification and sanctification because if δικαιοσύνη is the same as ἁγιασμός, then

---

[124] Maxwell, "Justification in the Early Church," 29–30. Maxwell's article is extremely helpful in looking at Cyril's understanding of justification from a number of angles. Not only does he identify Cyril's thinking on justification from his writings on John and Paul, but he also examines Cyril's understanding of concepts such as faith, free will, and *theosis*.

[125] Busenitz, *Long Before Luther*, 181. See also 241.

[126] Ibid., 134.

[127] Ibid., 181.

[128] Baker and Speidell, *T. F. Torrance and Eastern Orthodoxy*, 125.

δικαιοσύνη should not be translated as a "declared righteousness."[129] Morris confirms this distinction between δικαιοσύνη and ἁγιασμός by stating that in δικαιοσύνη "the forensic thought seems to underlie passages where righteousness is spoken of as a gift" and cites Rom 5:17; 9:30–32; and 2 Cor 5:21 for support.[130] The latter two references are particularly influential to him because if righteousness is a forensic gift "it cannot be a quality of living."[131] Contra Cyril, a distinction should be made between these terms for a correct understanding of these two key salvific terms because God, Scripture's ultimate author, was careful to use these two different terms to describe two different works that He is doing within His chosen people.

While δικαιοσύνη and ἁγιασμός are distinct terms, they are nonetheless inseparable. They have been referred to as "two legs of a pair of trousers."[132] Letham provides a comparative contrast to show the distinctions which is reproduced in table form below.[133]

| Justification | Sanctification |
| --- | --- |
| Removes guilt and condemnation | Overcomes the pollution of sin |
| One-time act, the same for all | Progressive act, not the same for all |
| Affects the believer's legal status | Affects the believer's moral status |
| Imputed | Imparted |
| The basis for eternal life | Prepares a believer for entering eternal life |

Letham continues, "We are not justified on the basis of our being transformed, but our transformation is grounded on our status as

---

[129] Baker and Speidell., 126.

[130] Morris, *The Apostolic Preaching of the Cross*, 275, 280–81.

[131] Ibid., 281.

[132] Letham, *Systematic Theology*, 736. In this instance, Letham is borrowing from Anthony N. S. Lane's description found in *Justification by Faith in Catholic-Protestant Dialogue* (London: T&T Clark, 2002), 18.

[133] Letham., 736.

righteous."[134] Another way of saying this would be that justification does not occur because we are transformed, but we are transformed because of our justification.

Grudem initially confuses the contrast between justification and sanctification by oversimplifying the differences. When he opens his chapter on sanctification, he provides a table contrasting justification and sanctification. But while rightly summarizing justification as "entirely God's work," he confusingly summarizes sanctification as something in which the believer cooperates.[135] While true in some contexts, it is only true in Scripture when it refers to the ongoing process experienced in the Christian life. Theologically this is understood as progressive sanctification (cf. Phil 2:12). As developed later in this book, sanctification can also describe initial salvation, which is entirely the work of God as well as describing final sanctification (glorification) which is also entirely the work of God.

It is noteworthy, then, to comprehend how Cyril viewed δικαιοσύνη and ἁγιασμός. He saw them as activities that God was producing salvifically in all believers. However, while Cyril saw that justification and sanctification were activities that God produces in each believer, he also saw in Scripture the participatory work of man. Despite these distinct positions, he did not attempt to distinguish between God's role and man's role. The result became a salvific synergism—a concept that would be developed more fully and espoused by Eastern Orthodoxy (as well as Roman Catholicism)[136] and Arminian theology. This synergistic thinking was later incorporated by some Protestant groups through the influence of Eastern Orthodox culture and literature. Stated differently, from Cyril's perspective, δικαιοσύνη (justification) and ἁγιασμός (sanctification) are activities that demonstrate a work initiated by God who has brought all who place their confidence in the gospel into union with Christ Jesus. While Cyril emphasized this monergistic

---

[134] Ibid., 737.

[135] Grudem, *Systematic Theology*, 746.

[136] Baker and Speidell, *T. F. Torrance and Eastern Orthodoxy*, 126.

concept, it is neither the emphasis of Eastern Orthodox theologians today nor what some Protestant theologians believe and teach today.

But Fairbairn goes on to develop how Cyril spoke of justification in his writings. Cyril uses the preposition ἐν to combine πίστει with δικαιοσύνη and δίκαίωσις. He uses δικαιοσύνη ἐν πίστει nine times and δίκαίωσις ἐν πίστει seventeen times to indicate that "God, Christ or grace is the direct source of our righteousness."[137] Additionally, Cyril uses the phrase "justified by faith" seventy-five times where the passive participle or passive infinitive of δικαιόω is used with πίστις to argue that the believer is receiving righteousness from outside himself. In Fairbairn's words, believers are "recipients of a righteousness that originates outside of ourselves, rather than being the producers of such righteousness."[138] This is a concept strongly associated with forensic justification.

To Cyril, an external righteousness received by faith alone was foundational to his understanding of God's spiritual work within the believer. Unfortunately, he did not make the proper distinction between δικαιοσύνη and ἁγιασμός, an error which led to him becoming one of the foundational, philosophical shapers of deification (θέωσις) that moved the Eastern Orthodox Church away from a forensic, reckoned understanding of justification to a sanative, infused understanding. This concept would later be adopted into some Slavic Protestant thinking through the portal of Eastern Orthodox literature.

Furthermore, Maxwell points out that Cyril integrated Hebrew and New Testament Scriptures in his understanding and definition of justification. Cyril does this by highlighting Paul's use of Abraham in his examples of forensic justification. Maxwell provides an example by citing Cyril's commentary on Romans. Cyril's citation from Rom 4:2 has only recently been translated into English and demonstrates he understands justification to be an attitude of forgiveness in the

---

[137] Ibid., 127.

[138] Baker and Speidell, *T. F. Torrance and Eastern Orthodoxy.*, 128.

mind of God and not an action by man that occurs in his heart.[139] Fairbairn confirms Cyril's synonymous association of δικαιοσύνη and ἁγιασμός by stating, "If one does not distinguish [δικαιοσύνη] from the holiness produced gradually in sanctification then one can hardly be said to espouse the Protestant understanding of justification."[140] Fairbairn earlier quoted Daniel Keating: "There is no marking off of justification from sanctification as distinguishable stages in our attainment of divine life" to establish his observation.[141] Unfortunately, Cyril's almost synonymous understanding of δικαιοσύνη and ἁγιασμός places forensic justification as part of the process of deification (θέωσις) rather than seeing "righteousness" as a forensic beginning, culminating in the final transformation at glorification as a result of seeing Jesus face-to-face (1 John 3:2).

There are other quotes from Patristic Fathers indicating they affirmed monergistic justification. Clement of Rome (d. ca. 100) said, "And so we, having been called through his will in Christ Jesus, are not justified through ourselves or through our own wisdom or understanding or piety, or works that we have done in holiness of heart, but through faith, by which the Almighty God has justified all."[142] In the *Epistle to Diognetus,* a second-century writing, the writer states,

> By what other one was it possible that we, the wicked and ungodly, could be justified, than by the Son of God? O sweet exchange! O unsearchable operation! O

---

[139] Maxwell, "Justification in the Early Church." 30–31. Maxwell cites Cyril's paraphrase of Rom 4:2: "Since Abraham honored the promiser by ascribing to him the power to accomplish all things, thus bearing witness to God, Abraham was justified (δεδικαίωται) before God and received a reward commensurate with an attitude of such devotion to God ... amnesty (ἀμνηστίαν) for the ancient charges."

[140] Baker and Speidell, *T. F. Torrance and Eastern Orthodoxy*, 126.

[141] Baker and Speidell., 125–26. Emphasis in the original. Keating observes that Cyril does not distinguish between justification and sanctification because he sees them both as an activity "flowing directly from God himself and as given to the Christian by God *from the outside*."

[142] Busenitz, *Long Before Luther*, 169.

benefits surpassing all expectation! That the wickedness of many should be hid in a single righteous One, and that the righteousness of One should justify many transgressors![143]

Irenaeus of Lyons (130–202) declared, "The Lord, therefore, was not unknown to Abraham, whose day he desired to see; nor, again, was the Lord's Father, for he had learned from the Word of the Lord and believed Him; wherefore it was accounted to him by the Lord for righteousness. For faith towards God justifies a man."[144] Ammonius (c. fifth century) was famous in his day as an Aristotelian commentator, an exegete of Plato, and teacher in Alexandria. He wrote in *Catena on the Acts of the Apostles 13.39*,

> It should be noted that those who believe in Christ are justified and obtain absolution from their sin. In fact, the Law of Moses was not unjust. Rather, it was difficult and able to justify only those who had followed the entire law perfectly. Therefore, it was clearly incapable of correcting people because the one who had fallen into a single crime was guilty of all. Thus, the law was not able to justify. And, since the law itself was incapable of justifying anyone, its inability to correct made people incapable of being justified by the precepts of the law.[145]

Many Patristic Fathers affirmed a monergistic justification by faith alone. Their understanding, although not overtly forensic, was implied. They recognized that righteousness originated outside themselves and was conferred upon the recipient by faith alone.

---

[143] Busenitz., 169–170.

[144] The Rev. Alexander Roberts and James Donaldson, eds., *The Apostolic Fathers with Justin Martyr and Irenaeus*, vol. 1, The Ante-Nicene Fathers (Grand Rapids: Eerdmans, 1973), 467.

[145] Martin, *ACTS*, 168.

But when did this implied forensic understanding of justification transition into a sanative, infused understanding? What was the mechanism influencing this change? A convincing case can be made by investigating Jerome. The question of when the understanding of justification as a forensic "declaration of righteousness" transitioned to sanative, infused understanding of "to be made righteous" as asserted by Roman Catholics, Eastern Orthodox, and much later by Arminian theologians is answered by saying it happened gradually, over time, beginning in the 4th century. Much of this change can be attributed to language differences between the Western and Eastern Churches. But it was aided specifically by Jerome's writings.

**Justification according to Jerome**

It appears that the Patristic Father Jerome (a contemporary of Augustine, Chrysostom, and Ambrosiaster) is a key personality in the transformation of δικαιοσύνη and δικαιόω from a forensic declaration to a sanative infusion of justification—especially in the Western Church. At first glance, Jerome would appear to be a strong proponent for forensic justification. In his writings, he makes strong statements defending justification by faith alone. In commenting on Rom 10:3 he says, "When an ungodly man is converted … God justifies by faith alone."[146] Furthermore, he states, "He who with all his spirit has placed his faith in Christ, even if he dies in sin, shall by his faith live forever."[147]

Busenitz adds to our knowledge of Jerome's rich collection of contributions regarding God's monergistic, declarative work in salvation. When Busenitz comments on Jerome's writings against Pelagius, he quotes Jerome as saying, "We are saved by grace rather than works, for we can give God nothing in return for what he has bestowed on us."[148] In his commentary on Ephesians, Jerome writes,

---

[146] Cited in Buchanan, *The Doctrine of Justification*, 95.

[147] Cited in Jacques Le Goff, *The Birth of Purgatory* (Chicago: The University of Chicago Press, 1984), 61.

[148] Busenitz, *Long Before Luther*, 178.

"[Paul] shows clearly that righteousness depends not on the merit of man, but on the grace of God, who accepts the faith of those who believe, without works of the Law."[149] Clearly defining justification as a forensic declaration does not appear to be foremost in the minds of our fourth-century Church Fathers. However, emphasizing God's monergistic work in salvation manifests itself in notables like Jerome, Augustine, and Cyril in their fight against Pelagian thinking.

However, Jerome is better known for his translation of the LXX and the Greek New Testament into the Latin language, known as the Vulgate. This translation is a major contributor to the theological misunderstanding of justification because Jerome used the Latin word *iustificare* and its word group in the translation of δικαιόω and its word group. The Latin word, however, does not carry the forensic idea of "to be declared righteous;" instead, the word group denotes the sanative idea of "to be made righteous."[150] This Latin concept slowly changed the understanding of later church thinking. Notice what some Old Catholics[151] are now saying today,

> Justification is a word used in scripture to mean that in Christ we are forgiven and actually made righteous in our living. Justification is not a once-for-all,

---

[149] Busenitz.

[150] E. A. Andrews, *Latin - English Lexicon* (NY: Harper & Brothers, 1877), n/a. It should be noted that Richard A. Muller's *Dictionary of Latin and Greek Theological Terms* (Grand Rapids: Baker, 1985) does state that *iustificatio* is defined as a legal declaration (pg. 162). However, he writes from a more theological rather than lexical perspective. Interestingly, Leo F. Stelten *(Dictionary of Ecclesiastical Latin,* [Peabody, MA: Hendrickson Publications, 2015], 312) who is Roman Catholic defines *iustitia* as "justice; a cardinal virtue whereby one gives to others that which is due them as a matter of right" confirming the Roman Catholic understanding of justification in a non-forensic sense. Similarly, Charlton T. Lewis who wrote *A Latin Dictionary* published by Clarendon Press in Oxford in 1879 and re-published in 1980 defined *iustifico* #1 as 'to act justly' and #2 as 'to make just' (pg. 1020).

[151] C. B. Moss, *The Old Catholic Movement, Its Origins and History* (London: SPCK, 1948), 1. Moss defines Old Catholics as "a group of self-governing national churches united by their acceptance of the Declaration of Utrecht (1889) as their dogmatic basis." It is a conservative revolt within Latin Christendom against the Papacy in the 19th century.

instantaneous pronouncement guaranteeing eternal salvation, regardless of how wickedly a person might live from that point on. Neither is it merely a legal declaration that an unrighteous person is righteous. Rather, justification is a living, dynamic, day-to-day reality for the one who follows Christ. The Christian actively pursues a righteous life in the grace and power of God granted to all who continue to believe in Him.[152]

This is a reaffirmation of the Council of Trent, which says, "If anyone says that the faith which justifies is nothing else but trust in the divine mercy, which pardons sins because of Christ; or that it is that trust alone by which we are justified: let him be anathema."[153] And again, "If anyone says that the sinner is justified by faith alone, meaning thereby that no other cooperation is required for him to obtain the grace of justification, and that in no sense is it necessary for him to make preparation and be disposed by a movement of his own will: let him be anathema."[154]

Notice that both the Council of Trent and the Old Catholics incorporate Cyril's conceptual understanding of the synonymous relationship between δικαιοσύνη and ἁγιασμός into the Latinized understanding of justification. The thinking of the Old Catholics reflects accurately the thinking of the modern-day Eastern Orthodox concerning justification.

One should not take issue with the above quotation in regard to living a life consistent with one's profession of faith. Evangelicals affirm with the Eastern Orthodox (and the Roman Catholic) Church

---

[152] Michael Nesmith, *The History and Beliefs of Old Catholicism* (Clarksville, TN: St. Michael's Old Catholic Seminary, 2004).

[153] James G. McCarthy, *The Gospel According to Rome* (Eugene, OR: Harvest House Publishers, 1995), 47. McCarthy quotes from Council of Trent, session 6, "Decree on Justification," canon 12.

[154] Ibid., 47. McCarthy quotes from Council of Trent, session 6, "Decree on Justification," canon 9.

that spiritual fruit is evidence of regeneration. Paul notes in Gal 5:22–25 that the new birth experience will be evidenced by the manifestation of the Holy Spirit's work in the life of the regenerate through love, joy, peace, patience, kindness, goodness, faithfulness, gentleness and self-control. Moreover, living the new birth experience is motivated out of gratitude for the divine regenerative work that will be expressed through obedience to the will of God (John 14:15; 1 John 2:3–5) —this will be developed later in this book when we examine how misunderstanding justification leads to the misunderstanding of grace (χάρις). Ultimately, this is a discussion of the difference between the relationship of faith and works before and after salvation.

But the issue in this discussion of justification regarding the quote above is the plain denial by the Old Catholics that justification is an instantaneous, once-for-all, legal declaration by God on behalf of the one professing faith in the finished work of Christ. This denial became the standard of thinking for both the Roman Catholic and Eastern Orthodox Churches and was incorporated into some Slavic Protestant thinking through their Eastern Orthodox cultural influence. This thinking would not be challenged with any degree of substance within the Roman Catholic Church until the beginning of the Reformation in 1517. But it was briefly challenged a little over 100 years later in Eastern Orthodoxy when forensic justification was introduced by Reformers as part of the attempt to unite the Reformed and Eastern Orthodox churches. However, the brief theological integration of forensic justification by the Eastern Orthodox Church did not have a lasting effect upon their theology.

### Justification Among the Reformers

No discussion on justification could be complete without an examination of the thinking of Luther (1483–1546) and Calvin (1509–1564)—the two most influential proponents of justification by faith alone during the Reformation.[155] Although there were

---

[155] John Piper, *Five Points: Towards a Deeper Experience of God's Grace* (Fearn, Scotland: Christian Focus Publications, 2017), 11.

forerunners who heralded a forensic view of justification by faith, it was Luther's internal struggles with his sin under the convicting influence of the Holy Spirit that led to his forensic, monergistic proclamations. Luther states,

> I greatly longed to understand Paul's Epistle to the Romans and nothing stood in my way but that one expression, "the justice of God," because I took it to mean that justice whereby God is just and deals justly in punishing the unjust. My situation was that, although an impeccable monk, I stood before God as a sinner troubled in conscience, and I had not confidence that my merit would assuage him. Therefore, I did not love a just and angry God, but rather hated and murmured against him. Yet I clung to the dear Paul and had a great yearning to know what he meant.
>
> Night and day I pondered until I saw the connection between the justice of God and the statement that "the just shall live by his faith." Then I grasped that the justice of God is that righteousness by which through grace and sheer mercy God justifies us through faith. Thereupon I felt myself to be reborn and to have gone through open doors into paradise. The whole of Scripture took on a new meaning, and whereas before the "justice of God" had filled me with hate, now it became to me inexpressibly sweet in greater love. This passage of Paul became to me a gate to heaven ...[156]

Luther highlights the joy of discovering that the justification from God comes from outside himself—a monergistic, forensic declaration and not a synergistic, sanative work. And he could not cease in his writings and lectures "exulting" over this external, outside

---

[156] Bainton, *Here I Stand*, 65.

himself act of God!¹⁵⁷ This kind of exulting in forensic justification is what I long to see in those under my ministry influence.

In commenting on Gal 2:16, Luther noted that faith in Christ's work justifies because it embraces and treasures Christ's work. He said, "Therefore the Christ who is grasped by faith and who lives in the heart is the true Christian righteousness, on account of which God counts us righteous and grants us eternal life."¹⁵⁸ This leads him to define a Christian as "a person not without sin but someone who because of faith in Christ, no longer is imputed with sin by God."¹⁵⁹ In the context of the comments on this verse, Luther is convinced that Paul is declaring that a Christian is one who has been freed from obtaining God's favor through legal obedience because only God, through Jesus' work on the cross, could provide the righteousness—forensically imputed by faith—that man needs. As a result, Luther was convinced that justification was central to religious and societal reform.¹⁶⁰

But did Luther make any clear statements that the δικαιόω word group referred to a monergistic, forensic declaration of righteousness? He frequently appealed to Augustine for support of his understanding on justification. As has been demonstrated, Augustine made no clear statements referring to a declarative, forensic meaning. As Luther began his study of Augustine in 1513, he believed in "progressive justification." After he began reading Augustine, Luther began to reject this thinking.¹⁶¹ This marked a clear shift in his belief on the doctrine of justification, providing clear, forensic statements in his commentary on Romans.

---

[157] See the discussion of καυχάομαι in the definition under the heading of "Grace" in Chapter 6 on page 94.

[158] Martin Luther, *Lectures on Galatians*, Luther's Works (St. Louis: Concordia, 1963), 130.

[159] Luther., 133.

[160] McGrath, *Historical Theology*, 161.

[161] Letham, *Systematic Theology*, 684.

Commenting on Rom 3:25, Luther says, "And all this God did 'to declare his righteousness' that is, to make it known that all men are sinners and in need of His righteousness."[162] He said this in the context of Rom 3:24, highlighting that God does not justify without atonement for sin but noting that God gave Jesus to atone for man's sins in order to propitiate (satisfy) His justice. Or, to say it conceptually in a similar way as Paul said it in Rom 3:25, faith in Christ's redemptive work was publicly displayed to mankind in order to highlight the righteous work of God that could only be conferred by a divine, forensic declaration.

Luther's transition to a forensic understanding of δικαιοσύνη and δικαιόω undid 1,100 years of the sanative development in Roman Catholic (and Eastern Orthodox) thinking. Luther used a Greek lexical argument as the foundation for his philosophical argument. This is an important contrast to the philosophical argument that was based upon a faulty Latin, lexical argument being used by his opponents.[163]

Melancthon and Luther influenced each other in their understanding of justification. Melancthon influenced Luther's competency of Greek. This is evidenced when Luther studied the language under Melancthon, who began teaching Greek literature at Wittenberg in August 1518.[164] On September 9, 1519, Melancthon wrote, "Therefore righteousness is the benefaction of Christ. All righteousness is the free imputation of God."[165]

Like Luther, John Calvin's understanding of justification had a strong, Greek lexical base. When commenting on Gal 2:16, Calvin

---

[162] Martin Luther, *Commentary on the Epistles to the Romans* (Grand Rapids: Kregel, 1978), 78.

[163] Wilhelm Pauck, *Luther: Lectures on Romans*, LCC (Philadelphia: Westminster Press, 1961), 18. Luther said, "The righteousness of God is that righteousness which he imparts in order to make men righteous."

[164] Lowell C. Green, "Faith, Righteousness, and Justification: New Light on Their Development Under Luther and Melanchton," *The Sixteenth Century Journal* 4, no. 1 (April 1973): 65–86.

[165] Green., 81.

said, "Men are justified by faith alone.... But Paul was unacquainted with the theology of the Papists, who declare that a man is justified by faith, and yet make a part of justification to consist of works. Of such half-justification Paul knew nothing."[166] Calvin argues that justification is monergistic and forensic, not synergistic and sanative—a synergism which he calls half-justification—a sanative synergism that the Roman Catholic system is built upon.

Calvin prefaced this comment on Gal 2:16 by noting that in Gal 2:15 Paul was very uneasy with anyone's hope being placed on performing ceremonies (a sanative approach) to the detriment of the gospel's glory.[167] It is reminiscent of Isaiah's statements in Isa 42:8 and 48:11 where God says He will not share His glory with anyone. Paul later describes the gospel in 1 Tim 1:11 as glorious. Philip Towner sees an "analogical function of the term 'glory' ... as descriptive of the gospel's content."[168] Calvin continued: "No mortal is justified by the righteousness of the law, the assertion amounts to this, that from such a mode of justification all mortals are excluded, and that no one can possibly reach it."[169] Further establishing a forensic base, when commenting on Gal 2:17, Calvin asserts "if, consequently, Christ is not sufficient for our righteousness, it follows that Christ is the minister of the doctrine which leaves men in sin."[170]

Furthermore, when commenting on Rom 3:25, Calvin affirms a Greek, forensic understanding of δικαιοσύνη and δικαιόω in contrast to the sanative interpretation by the Roman Catholic and Eastern Orthodox Churches. He says,

> And this definition or explanation again confirms what

---

[166] John Calvin, *Commentary on the Epistles of Paul to the Galatians and the Ephesians* (Grand Rapids: Baker, 2005), 69.

[167] Ibid., 68.

[168] Philip H. Towner, *The Letters to Timothy and Titus*, NICNT (Grand Rapids: Eerdmans, 2006), 132.

[169] Calvin, *Commentary on the Epistles of Paul to the Galatians and the Ephesians*, 70.

[170] Calvin, 71.

> I have already reminded you—that men are pronounced just, not because they are such in reality but by imputation: for he only uses various modes of expressions, that he might more clearly declare, that in this righteousness there is no merit of ours; for if we obtain it by the remission of sins, we conclude that it is not from ourselves; and further, since remission itself is an act of God's bounty alone, every merit falls to the ground.[171]

Calvin prefaced this quote by commenting on Rom 3:24, stating "Christ's obedience satisfied the Father's justice (*judicium*—judgment)."[172] Again, the forensic nature of justification is seen in work of Christ being conferred by declaration on the redeemed. In commenting on Rom 8:30, Calvin describes forensic justification as "gratuitous imputation," or a gift conferred by God and not an action by man rewarded by God.[173]

As noted earlier, although the Reformers frequently quoted Augustine and Cyril in defense of their forensic understanding of justification, these leaders did not infuse a sanative understanding with δικαιοσύνη and δικαιόω as did Cyril. Two thoughts were clear to the founders of the Reformation. First, justification was a forensic declaration by God. Second, there is a distinction between regeneration and sanctification.[174] The Reformers (until the time of Jacobus Arminius) were careful to maintain the forensic, lexical limitation on the word group.

The Reformers' return to the Greek, forensic understanding of

---

[171] John Calvin, *Commentary on the Epistles of Paul the Apostle to the Romans* (Grand Rapids: Baker, 2005), 144.

[172] Calvin, 141.

[173] Calvin., 319.

[174] Letham, *Systematic Theology*, 683–684.

δικαιόω was anathematized by the Council of Trent in 1547.[175] In Session 6, the Council wrote sixteen chapters and thirty-three canons to anathematize Luther's forensic understanding of justification.[176] Most glaringly, the Council declared the Vulgate to be an adequate translation for making the doctrinal proofs that resulted in anathematizing Luther's position. According to the *New Catholic Encyclopedia*, the supremacy of the Vulgate became clear in the sixth century and was established by the eight.[177] One of the goals of the Council of Trent was to establish the authority of the Vulgate, which they did in two decrees. Amazingly, the Roman Church is basing its authoritative doctrinal position for justification at the Council of Trent on an inferior translation (the Vulgate) rather than manuscripts in the original language of the New Testament.

### Justification Reintroduced to the Eastern Orthodox

The Eastern Orthodox Church had an opportunity to correct their thinking on justification in the early 1600s. At this time, the four regions of Eastern Orthodoxy (Constantinople, Alexandria, Antioch, and Jerusalem) were under the control of Muslims. The Eastern Church was in survival mode, looking for deliverance and under the control of a hostile religion. It was at this time that a young Greek priest named of Cyril Lukaris (1572–1638) was rising to prominence. He was born and raised on Crete, educated at an Orthodox school in Venice, and attended the University of Padua before teaching in Orthodox schools in Poland and Ukraine.[178] Later, he was attached to the Patriarchate of Constantinople and served as its representative in

---

[175] The Rev. A. Nampon, *Catholic Doctrine as Defined by the Council of Trent* (Philadelphia: Peter F. Cunningham & Son, 1869), 300–04.

[176] Nampon, The Rev. A., 304.

[177] L. F. Hartman, B. F. Peebles, and M. Stevenson, "Vulgate", *New Catholic Encyclopedia* (New York: Thomson Gale, 2003), 14:596.

[178] Protopresbyter Thomas Hopko, "The Orthodox Faith," in *Cyril Lukaris*, 1981, https://www.oca.org/orthodoxy/the-orthodox-faith/church-history/seventeenth-century/cyril-lukaris.

Brest (now a part of modern Belarus) beginning in 1596.[179]

The city of Brest and its region have a rich religious heritage influenced by Roman Catholics, Eastern Orthodox, and Protestants alike. The area was also the battleground between the Poles/Lithuanians (who were Roman Catholics) and Russians (who were Eastern Orthodox) for many centuries. The victor of the battles had control of religious thinking over the area. This area under the control of the Duchy of Lithuania was under the administrative rule of Mikolaj Radziwill (1515-1565).[180] Radziwill embraced the Calvinist faith and based upon Calvinistic principles implemented Calvinistic religious control. Once Radziwill died, however, all but one of his children converted to Catholicism and the area was again primarily under Roman Catholic influence.[181] The "seeds" of Protestantism, which had been planted in Slavic culture, were quickly "plucked up."

As noted above, this particular area experienced many religious reversals between Roman Catholicism and Eastern Orthodoxy. Cyril Lukaris was in Brest in 1596 (thirty-one years after the death of Radziwill) representing Constantinople in what became known as the Union of Brest.[182] Lukaris, representing Eastern Orthodoxy, was against this move. Some speculate that his strong hostility toward Roman Catholicism developed during this period. Though thirty-one years after the death of Radziwill and the subsequent erasure of his Calvinistic reforms, Lukaris could have been introduced to Protestant thinking during his brief time in Brest.

After returning to Constantinople, Lukaris' theological and leadership skills were recognized, resulting in his being elected

---

[179] Ware, *The Orthodox Church*, 96.

[180] *The New Encyclopaedia Britannica*, 15th ed., s.v. "Radziwill," 9:896.

[181] "The New Encyclopaedia Britannica.", 9:896.

[182] Ware, *The Orthodox Church,* 95. The Union of Brest was a document signed by many church leaders in the Duchy of Lithuania acknowledging the leadership of Rome in this territory.

Patriarch of Alexandria in 1601.[183] His patriarchate in Alexandria lasted until 1620 when he was elected Patriarch of Constantinople from 1620 to 1638. Upon being elected Patriarch of Constantinople, he focused on fighting Roman Catholic influence within the Ottoman Empire. The Ottomans controlled the Patriarchates of Eastern Orthodoxy. During this time, Lukaris attempted to enlist support for his work against Roman Catholic influence from the Protestant embassies in Constantinople, and it was during this time that he fully embraced Protestant theology.[184]

The Eastern Orthodox Church speculated that Lukaris embraced Calvinist thought because the flock of God under his care was suffering at the hands of the Ottoman Turks. Some speculate that he thought his "flock" would be encouraged by the enthusiasm of the Calvinist doctrines that were influencing Europe.[185] He published a distinctively Calvinistic statement of faith in 1629 for his Patriarchate in Constantinople. These Protestant reforms remained intact until his death in 1638, whereupon the Eastern Orthodox Church, in six councils between 1638 and 1691, condemned his thinking and returned to the traditional Eastern Orthodox position on justification.[186] His legacy within Eastern Orthodoxy is that he was as brilliant as Photius but marred by the political passions that destroyed his theology.[187]

### Slavic Baptist Thinking on Justification Under the Influence of Eastern Orthodoxy

There is an antipathy between Eastern Orthodox and Roman Catholic/Protestant relationships that has existed for centuries. It is not based exclusively on territorial control, but more importantly on

---

[183] Hopko, "The Orthodox Faith."

[184] Ware, *The Orthodox Church*, 96.

[185] Hopko, "The Orthodox Faith."

[186] Ware, *The Orthodox Church*, 96.

[187] Ibid.

theological ideas. Over time these theological differences have widened, and the Slavic Baptists are caught in the middle.

The modern Protestant movement began among the Eastern Slavs in the 1800s under the influence of John Paterson and Johann Oncken.[188] It was a small movement with limited access to Western Protestant thinking and much antagonism from the Eastern Orthodox.[189] And from 1917 to 1991, Eastern Slavic Baptists were isolated from Protestant thinking and influence and under the control religiously of an Eastern Orthodox culture in the midst of a Soviet, atheistic regime. This fact is crucial to understanding the Slavic Baptist position on justification by faith alone today.[190]

During the Soviet period of isolation from Western Protestant and Baptist influence, the Slavic Baptists—in the interest of survival—developed a religious relationship with the Eastern, and specifically Russian, Orthodox Church. This relationship developed because, under Soviet control, anyone calling themselves "Christian" was subjected to second-class citizenry and persecution.[191] In order to survive, the Orthodox and the Baptists temporarily partnered together and set aside doctrinal differences.

This relationship was doctrinally detrimental to the Slavic Baptists. As noted by Mark Harris, Slavic Baptists had neither their own self-written theological texts (they were dependent on others) nor

---

[188] More will be said about these two men in the following chapter.

[189] Mark J. Harris, "Historical Perspectives on the Evangelistic Theology and Methodology of Russian Baptists," 1999, http://cvi2.org/pages/harris/harris_russian_baptist_evangelistic_history_1999.pdf. 2.

[190] Sergiy S. Tarasenko, "The Historical And Doctrinal Influences of the Russian Orthodox Church on the Soteriology of the Russian Baptists" (unpublished ThM thesis, The Master's Seminary, 2004), 2. Tarasenko has done an excellent job in his ThM thesis of documenting what I have observed.

[191] Ware, *The Orthodox Church*, 145–160. Additionally, Tarasenko cites a Russian quote from Nikolay Kornilov stating that "Orthodox and Protestant Christians were in close cooperation with each other." This can be found on page 3 of his thesis.

did they have formal training to be pastors.[192] The result was a lack of a formalized, Baptist systematic theology. Without formal training and without Baptist theological resources, Baptist pastors were limited to the theological resources—when they could be found—available to them in the "closed" environment of the Soviet Union. Such theological resources most often were Eastern or Russian Orthodox. Subsequently, the model of salvation being incorporated into Slavic Baptist thinking was a synergistic work between God and man that flowed from an Orthodox model of deification (θέωσις) and excluded not only a monergistic model of justification but a forensic model as well. When F. George Florovsky, an Orthodox theologian and author, writes, "For Luther 'to justify'—dikaion—meant to declare righteous or just, not 'to make' righteous or just—it is an appeal to an extrinsic justice which in reality is a spiritual fiction,"[193] it is no surprise that the lexical study of δικαιόω and its word group as a forensic, *declarative* righteousness could be rejected (regrettably) by Slavic Baptist pastors.

The rejection of monergistic, forensic, declarative justification continues to be the standard of Eastern Orthodoxy today. In a pamphlet explaining the Eastern Orthodox theology, the unidentified author(s) define justification as

> a word used in the Scriptures to mean that in Christ we are forgiven and actually made righteous in our living. Justification is not a once-for-all, instantaneous pronouncement guaranteeing eternal salvation, no matter how wickedly a person may live from that point

---

[192] Harris, "Historical Perspectives on the Evangelistic Theology and Methodology of Russian Baptists." This information is found on page 5 of the download. Anecdotally, in private conversations with pastors in Belarus and Russia before the advent of Western missionaries many pastors were using Orthodox theological works to prepare their sermons.

[193] F. George Florovsky, "The Ascetic Ideal and the New Testament Reflections on the Critique of the Theology of the Reformation," n.d., http://www.romanity.org/htm/flo.01.en.the_ascetic_ideal_and_the_new_testament.01.htm. This work was first brought to my attention by Donald Fairbairn in his book *Eastern Orthodoxy Through Western Eyes* (Louisville, KY: Westminster, 2002), 92, footnote 48.

on. Neither is it merely a legal declaration that an unrighteous person is righteous. Rather, justification is a living, dynamic, day-to-day reality for the one who follows Christ. The Christian actively pursues a righteous life in the grace and power of God granted to all who are believing in Him.[194]

Notice the fusion of justification and progressive sanctification when a point-in-time declaration is rejected for the day-to-day, dynamic lifestyle of a believer. True, biblical orthodoxy understands justification to be a point-in-time declaration that is appreciated and motivates a day-to-day lifestyle rather than a day-to-day dynamic process leading to deification.

Slavic Baptists were fighting for survival in the midst of two giants—theistic Eastern Orthodoxy and atheistic Soviet rule. Today, the Slavic Baptists number no more than 9.4% of a country's population (Slovakia) and as few as .07% (Bosnia).[195] Of the thirteen nations represented by the Slavic Baptists, only two nations have Protestant populations above 1.88% —Ukraine with 3.8% and Slovakia with 9.4%.[196] In the eleven remaining countries, Slavic Baptists represent less than 2% of the population.[197] The gospel need in each country is immense. If Slavic Baptists are going to be effective representatives of God in Slavic countries where the need for the true gospel is great, then there is an even greater need to have properly

---

[194] *What Orthodox Christians Believe* (Ben Lemond, CA: Concilliar Press, 1988), 7.

[195] Jason Mandryk, *Operation World*, 7th ed. (Colorado Springs, CO: Biblica Publishing, 2010), 157, 747.

[196] Mandryk, Jason., 747, 844.

[197] Ibid., 749. Belarusian Protestants are represented by 131,000, or 1.36%, of the population (139); Bosnians by 3,000, or .07% (157); Bulgarians by 127,000, or 1.7% (173); Croatians by 23,000, or .52% (289); Czechs by 195,000, or 1.88% (298); Macedonians by 5,000, or .26% (546); Montenegrins by 3,000, or .1% (598); Poles by 169,000, or .44% (689); Russians by 1,750,000, or 1.24% (706); Serbians by 110,000, or 1.42% (735); and Slovenians by 22,000, or 1.1% (750).

defined biblical terms to properly convey biblical, soteriological concepts.

## Conclusion

There are at least three reasons that understanding justification as a sanative, on-going, synergistic work must be abandoned. First, forensic justification is the inherent, natural, lexical understanding of the δικαιόω word group. Its forensic nature is embedded in the Hebrew and Greek terms, and the heart of Pauline salvific theology in Romans and Galatians.

Second, this forensic, divine work is described by Paul as a one-time, judicial declaration with a continuing result by lexical meaning and Paul's use of the aorist tense. As a forensic term in both the Hebrew Scriptures and Greek New Testament writings, the emphasis is on the one-time declaration made by the judge in the verdict he renders. By using the aorist tense, which describes an established fact to picture the declaration made on the redeemed's behalf (cf. Rom 4:2; 5:1, 9; 8:30; Gal 2:16–17; Tit 3:7), Paul is stating an established truth that is a present reality. Justification, then, is not an affirmation to those who are trying really hard and hoping to please the judge with good efforts and good intentions over time. It is a one-time pronouncement that needs no improvement made by the judge to a guilty person in need of righteousness.

Third, this past, forensic work is a monergistic work of YHWH established by Paul in his use of the passive voice (cf. Rom 4:2; 5:1, 9; Gal 2:16–17; 3:24; Tit 3:7). The passive describes an outside action being performed on the subject. In each of the above referenced passages, the believer is the subject who is being acted upon monergistically by YHWH. This monergistic work in the past (from the believer's perspective), by a divinely, sovereignly, and legally conferred declaration, will result in future salvation.

The monergistic, divine action of justification was preserved in the thinking, preaching, and writing of the early Church Fathers. But as time progressed, there were two factors that contributed to the movement away from a monergistic, forensic understanding to a synergistic, sanative understanding of justification.

The first factor was the writings of some early Church Fathers, such as Cyril, who viewed justification as synonymous with sanctification despite being two different words with two distinctive concepts. Eastern churches, using a philosophical approach, synonymously combined justification and sanctification to develop the infused, sanative concept that became known as *deification* (θέωσις). This has had a compounding effect by redefining key terms, namely sanctification, salvation, grace, faith, and the concept of what it means to be created in the "image" and "likeness" of God (this will be developed in the following chapter). These redefinitions negatively affect the gospel of Jesus Christ. Although the Western church did not embrace deification, it nonetheless adopted a synergistic, infused, sanative approach to salvation. This thinking moved both churches—the Eastern and Western churches—away from the monergistic, forensic understanding of justification to a synergistic, infused, sanative one.

The second factor negatively impacting the biblical understanding of forensic justification occurred in the Western churches when Jerome translated the LXX and the New Testament from Greek into the Latin and used the *iustificare* word group as an equivalent to the δικαιόω word group. This appears to have "cemented" the idea of "being made righteous" into Western theological thinking until the time of the Reformation. The Reformers challenged the infused, sanative, Latin "being made righteous" definition of δικαιοσύνη and δικαιόω with a corrective, forensic, declarative way of thinking based upon the Greek definition of δικαιοσύνη and δικαιόω.

The Slavic Baptists, who have been influenced over the previous century by Eastern Orthodox theology, have been caught in the middle of the synergistic, sanative battle between Eastern Orthodoxy and Roman Catholicism as referenced earlier in connection with the Union of Brest in the 1500s. Although forensic justification had been introduced—albeit briefly—in the Eastern churches during the rule of Radziwill in the Duchy of Lithuania during the mid-1500s and again during the Patriarchy of Lukaris in Constantinople in the early 1600s, it was quickly and decisively overturned by Eastern Orthodoxy.

The challenge for the gospel facing the Slavic Baptist churches at the present is how to restore the forensic, lexical concepts of δικαιοσύνη and δικαιόω within a sanative, philosophical environment. It is not a simple corrective because Eastern Orthodoxy's philosophical approach makes it difficult to correctly define justification. As the next chapter will show, faulty and improper definitions (and, therefore, concepts) of justification have resulted in faulty and improper definitions and concepts of sanctification, salvation, grace, faith, and the concept of what it means to be created in the "image" and "likeness" of God.

# CHAPTER SIX

## THE EFFECT OF RE-DEFINING JUSTIFICATION

### The Effect of Redefining Justification on Other Salvific Terms

The redefinition of justification by Eastern Orthodoxy and Roman Catholicism from being "declared righteous" to "being made righteous" affects not only their understanding of "grace" and what it means to be created in the "image and likeness of God," it also has a snowball effect on other key salvific terms as well. Their understanding of "salvation," "sanctification," and "faith" have been dangerously impacted with an anathematizing result. This is the product of using a philosophical rather than lexical starting point to define biblical terms and concepts. Unfortunately, Eastern Orthodox influence has caused some Slavic Protestant thinking to move in a man-centered direction.

### The Effect of Redefining Justification on the Understanding of Salvation

Salvation can be described as faith in the divine act that delivers a sinner from the wrath of God and restores the person into a relationship with God.[198] The term salvation is often carelessly used to describe a religious event in an individual's life. When one believes the gospel, that person usually describes himself or herself as "being saved." The idea implied by this use of the term often is that they have been delivered from bad, present-life circumstances rather than from future, final judgment before God. For example, the gospel presentation many have heard begins by stating "God loves you and has a wonderful plan for your life!." The concept of salvation becomes associated with a past experience that will keep one from present and future temporal difficulties. While this may indeed be the experience of some, Jesus indicated something different. He warned

---

[198] John MacArthur and Richard Mayhue, *Biblical Doctrine: A Systematic Summary of Biblical Truth* (Wheaton, IL: Crossway, 2017), 936.

His audiences to expect more temporal difficulties as a result of following Him (e.g., Matt 5:10–12). In fact, a more careful study of σώζω (*sōzō*) and the word group's usage in the New Testament reveals a richer concept than many Christians—especially new Christians—are taught.

Werner Foerster and Georg Fohrer explain that σώζω was used in Hellenistic literature to describe "an acutely dynamic act in which gods or men snatch others by force from serious peril."[199] *NIDNTTE* agrees by noting that in religious and philosophical contexts σώζω refers to gods saving "mortals from various perils of life."[200] To be saved means to be acted upon by an outside force that delivers one from some form of acute danger. In a New Testament religious context, it is not the force or action of a man that delivers himself from the wrath of God for his sin but the action of God whereby God delivers a man from His future wrath coming upon man.[201] Eastern Orthodox theologians, and in many cases members of Slavic Protestant churches, are not aware of or do not emphasize this understanding of this common New Testament term.

But there is an even greater understanding of the word σώζω that is frequently overlooked in Christian thinking—its multi-faceted time component. The Pastoral Epistles use σώζω in three diverse ways: to describe past, present, and future realities.[202] The primary concept associated with σώζω is the monergistic divine work of "deliverance" from experiencing God's future wrath (Mark 10:26; Rom 5:9; 1 Cor 3:15; 5:5; 1 Thess 5:9–10). The concept of hope is attached to σώζω—a confident hope in Jesus's monergistic work on the cross that will deliver the sinner from the *future* wrath of God.

---

[199] *TDNT*, "σώζω,"7:966.

[200] *NIDNTTE*, "σώζω," 4:420.

[201] Sakae Kubo, *A Reader's Greek-English Lexicon of the New Testament and a Beginner's Guide for the Translation of New Testament Greek* (Grand Rapids: Zondervan, 1975), 277. Kubo notes that σώζω is used 106 times in the NT.

[202] *NIDNTTE*, "σώζω ," 4:420.

When it is used to describe a *present* reality, it is really describing sanctification—the present synergistic divine and human work in a justified sinner for progressive, behavioral transformation (Phil 2:12, 13).

When it describes a *past* experience, it is more proper to use the term δικαιόω ("to be justified;" cf. Rom 5:10).

These three conceptual time components have not been fully developed or distinguished in the Slavic Protestant context—to have been saved (monergistically) in the past (i.e., justified), to be being saved synergistically in the present (more properly described as the progressive sanctification of the one already trusting in God's rescue from future wrath), and to be promised to be saved (monergistically) from future wrath (i.e., glorification).

Compounding the problem is the lack of understanding the monergistic and synergistic components of salvation. As a result, the fully synergistic approach advocated by Eastern Orthodoxy is incorporated into some Slavic Protestant thinking on past, present, and future salvation.

## The Effect of Redefining Justification the Understanding of Sanctification and Salvation

As mentioned earlier, Cyril of Alexandria used δικαιοσύνη and ἁγιασμός as virtually synonymous terms. But the most basic understanding of language shows that a synonymous relationship between δικαιοσύνη and ἁγιασμός cannot be sustained because of the vast difference in their lexical meaning. "To be declared righteous" (the Greek meaning of the δικαιόω word group[203]) is vastly different than "to bring into a close relationship by separating oneself" from the world to God (the Greek New Testament meaning of the ἁγιάζω word group).[204]

The noun ἁγιασμός describes the continuous action of the

---

[203] *NIDNTTE*, "δικαιοσύνη", 1:725, 735.

[204] *EDNTW*, "Sanctification, Sanctify," 3:317.

believer in this life who is separating himself from worldly, ungodly behavior as a course of life (1 Thess 4:3, 7; Rom 6:19, 22; 2 Cor 3:18; 7:1). Vine describes this activity in the NT as either a "separation to" God (see Acts 20:32; Rom 15:16) or a "separation from" evil or the world (see John 17:17, 19).[205] This is called progressive sanctification, which is defined as a gradual transformation in this life (a process that will never be complete in this life).[206] Christians set aside (separate from) behavior displeasing to the God who has redeemed them in order to honor God by conforming to (that is, to separate unto) the image of Jesus, the one who purchased them with His blood (Col 3:10).

Vine states that progressive sanctification is not vicarious but a learned behavior that is "an individual possession built up little by little, as the result of obedience to the Word of God, and of following the example of Christ."[207] Jesus taught His disciples to pursue obedience as His followers in an act of love to honor Him (John 14:15, cf. 1 John 2:3–5). In an analogous way, Jesus taught His disciples to learn from Him—that is, copy His example of living—as His followers (Matt 11:29). He then, in John 13:15, demonstrated an example He desired His disciples to learn. In one of His final messages to the disciples before His crucifixion, He served them by washing their feet as an example of what He wanted them to learn and duplicate (John 13:15). Thus, the pursuit of sanctification in this life is a progressive conformity to the behavioral example of Jesus as an expression of love for being justified through faith alone rather than being a process of making personal improvements resulting in union with God as taught by the Eastern Orthodox.

While the Eastern Orthodox Church acknowledges that sanctification is the act of "being set apart for God," there are two examples that demonstrate the damage they have done to the gospel by redefining this concept. First, they go beyond the scriptural

---

[205] *EDNTW*, "Sanctification, Sanctify," 3:317.

[206] Grudem, *Systematic Theology*, 750.

[207] *EDNTW*, "Sanctification, Sanctify," 3:317.

definition of the words by saying sanctification "involves us in a process of being cleansed and made holy by Christ in the Holy Spirit."[208] There is a deviation from the biblical concept in their phrase to be "made holy" by Christ and the Holy Spirit. Justification means to be "declared" righteous (or holy) in the sight of God. Ultimately, being made righteous or holy" does not occur until believers see Jesus (1 John 3:2). Cyril's fusion of the meanings of justification and sanctification can here be seen in the Eastern Orthodox definition.

Second, the Eastern Orthodox definition of sanctification says: "We are called to be saints…. We cooperate with God, we work together with Him, that we may know Him, becoming by grace what He is by nature."[209] Scripture does not say that Christians are "called to be saints" or "becoming saints" (implying a process to become one). Instead, believers are simply identified as "saints" as the product of their justification (cf. 1 Cor 1:2; Eph 1:1; Phil 1:1).

As already noted, the primary concept associated with σώζω is the monergistic divine work of "deliverance" from experiencing God's future wrath (Mark 10:26; Rom 5:9; 1 Cor 3:15; 5:5; 1 Thess 5:9–10). The concept of hope is attached to σώζω—a confident hope in Jesus's monergistic work on the cross that will deliver the sinner from the *future* wrath of God.

Again, as already noted, it describes a past, divinely initiated, monergistic, faith event that is used to describe a believer's present confidence which secures his future of acceptance in the eternal presence of God. While this use of 'being saved' is an accurate description of his past spiritual life event that has a continuing effect, it would be more biblically accurate to use the biblical term justified

---

[208] No author, *What Orthodox Christians Believe*, 7. Their full definition of sanctification is: "Sanctification is being set apart for God. It involves us in the process of being cleansed and made holy by Christ and the Holy Spirit. We are called to be saints and grow into the likeness of God. Having been given the gift of the Holy Spirit, we actively participate in sanctification. We cooperate with God, we work together with Him, that we may know Him, becoming by grace what He is by nature."

[209] Ibid.

("He has been justified by God and, as a result, he has the present joy of looking forward to being saved from experiencing the eternal wrath of God"; cf. Rom 5:10).

Third, the most problematic usage of the σῴζω word group comes in describing a present experience that is better described as "progressive sanctification." Paul writes in Phil 2:12[210] that believers should "work out your salvation with fear and trembling," giving the appearance that salvation is an ongoing, synergistic process in this life. Without a biblical understanding of justification, one would be inclined to think one would need to embrace a present, working process to secure God's favor before one ends this life in order to enter into eternity with God's favor and support.

It is worth repeating that these three conceptual time components have not been fully developed or distinguished in the Slavic Protestant context, that is, to have been saved (monergistically) in the past (i.e., justified), to be being saved synergistically in the present (more properly described as the progressive sanctification of the one already promised by God to be rescued from His future wrath), and to be promised to be saved (monergistically) from future wrath (i.e., glorification).

As a result, salvation should be properly viewed from three vantage points. Primarily, salvation should be viewed as deliverance from God's future wrath. Secondarily, salvation can be used by believers in the place of justification to describe their confidence at the present time in God's past declaration. Thirdly, salvation can be seen as an aspect of God's salvific work known as progressive sanctification.

In contrast, Eastern Orthodoxy teaches that salvation is a *progressive process* in order to deliver a person from God's future wrath—a teaching which has influenced some Slavic Protestants. The Bible teaches no such process for salvation. Paul emphatically teaches that confidence in the sufficiency of Jesus' work on the cross results in God's salvation (more accurately described as His *declaration of*

---

[210] MacArthur and Mayhue, *Biblical Doctrine,* 638. MacArthur and Mayhue cite Phil 2:12–13 and 2 Cor 3:18 as the two foundational texts clarifying this truth.

*righteousness* aka justification. This declaration launches the one exhibiting such faith on a journey of *progressive sanctification* in this life. This pursuit by *the declared righteous sinner* is an expression of appreciation in their confidence of the sufficiency they have in the work of Christ while they confidently wait for their ultimate sanctification (glorification). God did not design a process for being declared or accepted as righteous—He provided a confident expectation through the promise He made for which the justified *(declared righteous)* sinner is waiting to be fulfilled.

## Identifying Eastern Orthodox Theological Concepts in Slavic Protestant Thinking

The theological consequences for departing from the proper definitions of words in the original languages are significant. In particular, using the Latin word *iustificare* as the equivalent for the Greek word δικαιόω in the fourth century had long-lasting effects. In the Western Church, it changed the focus from a forensic declaration of justification to an infused, sanative understanding.

The Eastern Church used a more philosophical approach to arrive at its sanative understanding of justification. This was more than likely aided in the fourth century by Cyril's association of δικαιοσύνη and ἁγιασμός as virtually synonymous terms as they developed their concept of deification (θέωσις). This action by the Eastern churches also had a snowball effect on other key theological terms like sanctification, salvation, grace, faith, and the "image" and "likeness" of God.

The movement from a forensic to a sanative understanding of justification in both the Western and Eastern churches has had a devastating effect on the understanding of the gospel. Over the past 2,000 years of Christian theological expression, the redefinition of justification diverted the Eastern and Western churches from a God-centered to a man-centered understanding of salvation. The Reformation was a corrective measure to redirect the Church towards a God-centered focus of the gospel. But this was a helpful measure in only the Western Church among the Protestants. And even this change was challenged early in the Protestant movement by men like Jacob Arminius who emphasized a more man-centered, sanative approach in their teaching. This man-centered focus continues among many Protestants world-wide today which is remarkably similar to Eastern Orthodox thinking. Although corrective changes to a more God-centered focus of the gospel were temporarily introduced into the Eastern Church by a few of their leaders in partnership with Reformers during the 1600s, they were quickly reversed at the earliest opportunity.

Although strongly Calvinistic since their start in the early 1800s, Eastern Slavic Baptists have been primarily under the theological influence of Eastern Orthodoxy because it has been the dominant, Slavic cultural influence since 988 AD when Prince Vladimir embraced Eastern Orthodoxy and made it the state religion.[211] During the Soviet Era of 1917–1989, Slavic Baptists were isolated from Western Protestant churches, and consequently, from Reformation principles. During the Soviet era, Slavic Baptist theology more readily adopted the man-centered thinking of Eastern Orthodoxy at the expense of biblical, God-centered teaching. How does the consequence of Eastern Orthodox theological thinking manifest itself among the Slavic Baptists? This will be the focus of the next chapter.

---

[211] Ware, *The Orthodox Church*, 78.

# CHAPTER SEVEN
# THE EFFECT OF RE-DEFINING JUSTIFICATION ON THE CONCEPT OF GRACE

## Grace

Grudem defines grace in general as "the goodness of God toward those who deserve only punishment."[212] Notice it is a one-way, divine action extended on a Divinely chosen recipient. But this general definition must be more carefully separated into what theologians call common grace and efficacious grace. Common grace describes the blessings conferred by God upon all people whether they are saved or not.[213] Efficacious grace describes those who have been chosen by God to experience His salvation.[214]

We must also biblically define efficacious grace because χάρις (*charis*, "grace") is the central Pauline "concept that most clearly expresses his understanding of the salvation event."[215] W. E. Vine summarizes χάρις well, noting that χάρις has an objective sense and a subjective sense in the New Testament.[216] According to its objective sense, χάρις bestows "favorable regard" and is exemplified in Luke 2:40, where Jesus's growth in wisdom is evidence that the "grace" ("favor") of God was upon Him.[217] Berkhof notes that this is the "more prominent meaning of the word."[218] *NIDNTTE* concurs and notes that its objective sense "is often used of the concrete favor or

---

[212] Grudem, *Systematic Theology*, 1243.

[213] Grudem., 1238.

[214] MacArthur and Mayhue, *Biblical Doctrine*, 927.

[215] *TDNT,* "χάρις," 9:393.

[216] *EDNTW*, "Grace," 2:169–70.

[217] Ibid., 2:170.

[218] Louis Berkhof, *Systematic Theology* (Grand Rapids: Eerdmans, 1977), 427.

act of kindness bestowed on someone."[219] Because "grace" simply means "favor," MacArthur and Mayhue note that inherent in the meaning is the concept that it is bestowed without any basis of merit on the part of the recipient.[220]

It (χάρις, *charis*, "grace") can also describe the subjective effect of this kindness on the part of one who has experienced it. *NIDNTTE* describes grace as "that which brings well-being" or a "source of joy."[221] Romans 5:2 is such an example, where the believer's justification is an expression of God's χάρις ("favor") through faith in the work of Christ (cf. also Rom 3:24).

There are two important clarifications related to the objective element of χάρις. First, it is the action of bestowal or the act of giving. The word χάρις includes the sense of a gift being given to another. Second, the act of giving is done with a favorable attitude toward the recipient.

In its subjective sense, χάρις emphasizes the friendly, spontaneous character of the one bestowing a gift that is designed for the joy or pleasure of the recipient. For example, it is used in Rom 4:16 to contrast the "grace" ("favor") of God received by the obedience of faith rather than obedience to the law. The subjective element that should be remembered is that the gift is designed to bring joy and pleasure *in* the recipient. The joy *in* the recipient is God's design for the response to grace resulting in justification and is more fully developed by Paul in Rom 5:1–11. Being justified by grace through faith should manifest itself in exultation (καυχάομαι) by the justified (cf. vv. 2, 3, and 11).

Paul uses the word καυχάομαι (NASB "exult") to describe the recipient's subjective response of God's bestowed favor through faith alone. The verb καυχάομαι is used thirty-seven times in the New Testament, with five of those references found in Romans—three

---

[219] *NIDNTTE*, "χάρις," 4:653.

[220] MacArthur and Mayhue, *Biblical Doctrine*, 182.

[221] *NIDNTTE*, "χάρις," 4:653.

times in 5:1–11. The word has been translated variously in that context as "exult" (NASB), "rejoice" (ESV, KJV), and "boast" (NIV), but none of these translations conveys the fullness of the Greek or its implication in the context of Romans 5 as it relates to our understanding of justification by grace through faith.

The word is also inconsistently translated by the major English translations throughout the rest of the New Testament. The NASB, ESV, NIV, and KJV usually translate καυχάομαι as "boast" (although the NIV translates the word as "take pride" in 2 Cor 5:12 and Jas 1:9). The ESV translates the word as "glory" in Phil 3:3, and the KJV translates the word as "glory" in 1 Cor 1:29; 3:21; 4:7; 2 Cor 5:12; 11:12; 11:18; 12:9; Gal 6:14, but as "rejoice" in Phil 3:3 and Jas 1:9. In Rom 5:2, 3, and 11, the ESV consistently translates it as "rejoice," while the KJV uses "rejoice" (v. 2), "glory" (v. 3) and "joy" (v. 11), and the NIV translates καυχάομαι as "boast" in verses 2 and 11 but as "glory" in verse 3. It is a difficult word to translate into English, let alone Russian. Only the NASB consistently translates καυχάομαι as "exult."

The word καυχάομαι is best translated as "to boast" and is primarily used in a negative sense![222] In the New Testament it is almost exclusively Pauline. It can express legitimate pride and can warn against self-glory. But it can also be used in a positive sense to describe the boasting of a man who finds his justification in the work of Christ. This is the sense in which Paul uses καυχάομαι in Rom 5:2, 3, and 11. It is in this sense that we see the objective and subjective elements of χάρις come together. God has designed a gift of favor that will bring joy to the recipient when His gift is received and results in a welling up of joy within the recipient that must—and will be—expressed outwardly, openly, and publicly! Regrettably, this is rarely seen in Slavic Baptist or Eastern Orthodox churches, probably due to a lack of understanding regarding this rich word combined with a merit-based theological leaning.

Thus, the grace of God in justification contains both an

---

[222] *TDNT*, "καυχάομαι," 3:646.

objective and subjective element. God's grace in justifying a sinner is His friendly, favorable regard that He designed to be experienced with joy or pleasure within His chosen recipient, or, as Conzelmann and Zimmerli note, it is the linguistic starting point for understanding that grace is the sense of "making glad by gifts."[223] In this regard, it is all the more important to understand why this boasting in justifying grace is founded on faith rather than works. If it takes place as the result of one's own merit, then this boasting is in one's own efforts. But if this boasting in based on the efforts of another and undeservedly received as a result of faith (or confidence) in the effectiveness (efficacy) of that effort, then the boasting is not in one's self-effort but in the efficacious effort of the conferee. However, this is not the understanding of grace employed by Eastern Orthodoxy, as will be seen below. More importantly, this redefinition of grace by Eastern Orthodoxy has influenced a significant part of Slavic Protestant thinking.

## Preliminary Thoughts on the Eastern Orthodox Understanding of
### the Relationship between χάρις and δικαιοω

Why is Eastern Orthodox thinking so often different from biblical thinking? The Eastern Orthodox do not use the traditional, lexical definitions of the Koine Greek terms used in the New Testament or LXX to define their theological understanding of these biblical terms. Instead, they redefine the terms philosophically. For instance, Bishop Kallistos of Diokleia describes his book as "a clear, detailed introduction to the Orthodox Church written for the non-Orthodox as well as for Orthodox Christians who wish to know more about their own tradition."[224] He commits to defining and explaining Eastern Orthodoxy. When reading his book, one finds that he does this philosophically and he does it well.

Bishop Kallistos knows Orthodoxy. He was born in Bath,

---

[223] *TDNT,* "χάρις," 9:394.

[224] Ibid., front cover.

England in 1934. He joined the Orthodox Church in 1958 and was ordained a priest in 1966 (receiving the name Kallistos). Since that time, he has been a Spalding lecturer at Oxford on Eastern Orthodox studies and has served as the pastoral charge over the Greek parish in Oxford. He became a Fellow of Pembroke College at Oxford in 1970 and in 1982 was consecrated as Bishop of Diokleia and assistant Bishop of the Orthodox Archdiocese of Thyateira and Great Britain. He has authored many books on Eastern Orthodoxy.[225]

In his book, *The Orthodox Church,* Bishop Kallistos wrestles with the question of how humans can know an unknowable God without assuming the divine essence, basing his inquiry upon the Eastern Orthodox understanding of 2 Pet 1:4.[226] He suggests that the problem was solved by Gregory Palamas (1296–1359), who said that while man cannot know or partake in the essence of deity, he is able to partake in the energies of deity.[227] The energies of God are an important concept to understand if one wants to understand the influence of Eastern Orthodoxy on Slavic Baptist theology.[228]

Since 2 Pet 1:4 is the chief biblical reference upon which Eastern Orthodoxy bases its understanding of deification (θέωσις), a few words of clarification are in order. The Eastern Orthodox Church affirms that deification is an ancient theological term used to describe

---

[225] Ware, Timothy, *The Orthodox Church.*, Front matter.

[226] Ware, Timothy., 67.

[227] Ware, Timothy., 68.

[228] Georgios I. Mantzaridis, *The Deification of Man* (Crestwood, NY: St. Vladimir's Seminary Press, 1984), 17. The Eastern Orthodox put earnest effort into making a distinction between the *essence* of God and the *energies* of God. It is a philosophical distinction that began with Gregory Palamas who has been referenced consistently in their discussion on the *essence* and *energies* of God and is connected to a discussion of what it means to be created in the *image* and *likeness* of God. However, as will be demonstrated below under the heading of "A Related Issue: Image and Likeness," the philosophical approach comes at the expense of the lexical meanings not only of *image* and *likeness*, but ultimately of other biblical terms like *grace, faith, salvation, sanctification,* and *justification.*

the process undertaken by the believer to become more like God.[229] The Eastern Orthodox Church base this claim on an interpretation of Peter's phrase in 2 Pet 1:4 wherein Peter speaks of becoming "partakers of the divine nature." While they rightfully say that this does not mean that "human beings become divine" in essence,[230] they believe humanity (because man is made in God's image) can become more like God through His grace or divine *energies*. What Eastern Orthodoxy means by the *energies* of God is developed in the next section. For now, we need to note that the Eastern Orthodox Church claims "partaking in the divine nature" is the process of becoming more like God over an extended period of time through the *energies* of God.[231] But is this what Peter is saying in 2 Pet 1:4?

Michael Green notes that the phrase "partakers of the divine nature" was an often-used phrase in Peter's Day. It can be found in the writings of Philo, Stobaeus and Josephus.[232] The Stoics taught that men could become like gods by nature while the Platonists taught that man could become like gods through law.[233] It was a well-known concept in Peter's day, and both Green[234] and Kistemaker[235] affirm that Peter is infusing a distinctively Christian meaning to the term. Green argues that Peter is "putting his Christian doctrine in Greek dress" as an assault on Hellenistic thinking.[236]

But what is the biblical truth Peter is attempting to

---

[229] St. Athanasius Academy of Orthodox Theology, *The Orthodox Study Bible* (Nashville: Thomas Nelson, 2009), 1694.

[230] St. Athanasius Academy of Orthodox Theology., 1694.

[231] Ware, *The Orthodox Church,* 232–38.

[232] Michael Green, *The Second Epistle of Peter and the Epistle of Jude*, TNTC Vol 18 (Grand Rapids: Eerdmans, 1979), 24.

[233] Green., 25.

[234] Green., 24.

[235] Simon J. Kistemaker, *Peter and Jude,* NTC (Grand rapids: Baker, 1988), 248.

[236] Green, *The Second Epistle of Peter and the Epistle of Jude,* 24–25.

communicate? The structure of the sentence in 2 Peter 1:4, as noted by MacArthur,[237] Green,[238] and Kistemaker,[239] focuses on the promises of God mentioned in verse four. Kistemaker says, "The promises themselves are an important part of this verse."[240] All three commentators note that it is the promises of God that allow believers to participate in the divine nature. MacArthur[241] and Kistemaker[242] highlight Peter's use of the perfect tense of the word "granted" as one seeks to understand this phrase by Peter. The perfect tense emphasizes something that happened in the past with continuing results. This alone should discount the Eastern Orthodox interpretation of this verse, since their interpretation exchanges the concept of a past completed event with ongoing results for an ongoing process that eventually produces results.

But additional observations of the text produce a fruitful refutation of the Eastern Orthodox viewpoint. Kistemaker states that 2 Pet 1:3 and 2 Peter 1:4 are closely tied together[243] and MacArthur ties the two verses together through the complimentary usage of the word "granted."[244] In verse 3, the "divine power" has "granted" everything pertaining to (spiritual) life and godliness. Note that the word "granted" is a perfect passive emphasizing a past action with ongoing results performed by someone other than the subject (in the context, identified as God) that benefits the subject (in the context, identified as Christians). In verse four, the "promises" have granted

---

[237] John MacArthur, *2 Peter & Jude*, MacNTC (Chicago: Moody Press, 2005), 30.

[238] Green, *The Second Epistle of Peter and the Epistle of Jude,* 64.

[239] Kistemaker, *Peter and Jude,* 248.

[240] Kistemaker., 247.

[241] MacArthur, *2 Peter & Jude,* 30.

[242] Kistemaker, *Peter and Jude,* 247.

[243] Ibid., 247.

[244] MacArthur, *2 Peter & Jude,* 30.

the subjects (Christians) "to partake in the divine nature" (a perfect middle emphasizing a past action with ongoing results personally being performed on the subject [Christians] by an outside being [God]). In both verses the subject is the believer who is completely equipped spiritually for both the present and the future (verse 3) through the work of Jesus.[245] Kistemaker, furthermore, notes that using "granted" in the perfect tense implies that God has not only given but fulfilled His promises in Christ.[246] Peter, then, is telling us of the present and future benefits that all believers began enjoying when they expressed faith in the gospel.

But what does it mean that the believer partakes or participates in the divine nature? Kistemaker points out that anyone who exegetes Scripture is in partial agreement with the Eastern Orthodox who say, "we can never participate in God's essence."[247] He points out that Peter states believers share in God's *nature*, not His *being*. To share a *nature* with someone indicates the growth, development, and character of a person. Sharing in someone's *being* points to sharing the natural essence or substance of that person.[248] The creation can never share in essence what is natural in the Divine. Peter is not saying that believers will ever share in the divine essence.

But what is God sharing with His redeemed? In its most general sense, Peter is describing the benefits of sharing or participating in the divine nature, which include escaping the effects of the world's corruption, including the final destruction.[249] More specifically, in the Greek, the word partake is κοινωνοὶ. This term connotes "to have in common" or "to partake."[250] MacArthur

---

[245] MacArthur., 30. See also Green, *The Second Epistle of Peter and the Epistle of Jude,* 64.

[246] Kistemaker, *Peter and Jude,* 247.

[247] Kistemaker, *Peter and Jude,* 248.

[248] Kistemaker.

[249] MacArthur, *2 Peter & Jude,* 31.

[250] *EDNTW,* "Partake, Partaker," 3:161.

interprets this as believers partnering in the life that belongs to God.[251] Green says it conveys that believers become participants in the divine family.[252] Kistemaker stresses it describes sharing in God's holiness.[253] The one thing in which they all agree is that believers share in the promises of God both presently and in the future—promises that were conferred in the past through grace but are not being earned in the present time or over time. MacArthur says it well: "Believers are in this life partners in the very life that belongs to God."[254] Kistemaker reminds us that participating in the life that belongs to God carries the responsibility to reflect His virtues.[255]

## What Does Eastern Orthodoxy Mean by the *Energies* of God?

According to Eastern Orthodoxy, partaking in the energies of God occurs when a person enters into, or begins, the process of deification. The Eastern Orthodox do not use the term salvation, but rather employ the term "deification" or "theosis" (θέωσις) to combine and describe the religious process and experience of redemption and sanctification that eventually leads a person to salvation.[256] Mantzaridis states the Eastern Orthodox understanding of deification by saying, "The Spirit does not actually bring about man's deliverance but gives him access to the regenerative and divine work of Christ that has been accomplished once for all."[257] The phrase "accomplished once for all," from the Eastern Orthodox perspective, refers to the work of Christ putting the believer on the path toward

---

[251] MacArthur, *2 Peter & Jude,* 30.

[252] Green, *The Second Epistle of Peter and the Epistle of Jude,* 64.

[253] Kistemaker, *Peter and Jude,* 248.

[254] MacArthur, *2 Peter & Jude,* 31.

[255] Kistemaker, *Peter and Jude,* 248.

[256] Ware, *The Orthodox Church,* 231.

[257] Mantzaridis, *The Deification of Man,* 15.

deification rather than a sufficient, forensic declaration of accomplishment. This will be more fully developed in the next section.

From the Eastern Orthodox perspective, according to Bishop Kallistos, "God enters into a direct and immediate relationship with humankind" through His energies.[258] He continues, "The divine energy is in fact nothing else than the grace of God."[259] From the Eastern Orthodox perspective, when God dispenses His grace, He is dispensing His energies so man can accomplish his own deification or theosis.

There is much to unpack in Bishop Kallistos's description, but it should be noticed that Eastern Orthodoxy does not define grace lexically; rather, it defines it philosophically. The lexical meaning of χάρις (grace) as God intended it to be understood in His inspired word is ignored and replaced with a philosophical meaning.

## A Related Issue: Being Created in the Image and Likeness of God

To better understand this redefinition of grace and its impact on the Eastern Orthodox understanding of salvation with its influence upon the Slavic Protestants, one must also understand the Eastern Orthodox concept of what it means to be created in the image and likeness of God. Once again, Eastern Orthodoxy does not accept the lexical definitions of the biblical terms. The meanings of the Hebrew words for image (צֶלֶם) and likeness (דְּמוּת) are ignored and replaced with philosophical ones.

The basic meaning of image (צֶלֶם) describes something that is cut out.[260] It describes a carved or crafted, three-dimensional, physical representation of something in reality.[261] It expresses the idea of

---

[258] Ware, *The Orthodox Church*, 68.

[259] Ibid., 68.

[260] *BDB*, צֶלֶם, 853.

[261] *NIDOTTE*, "Form, Image", 4:646.

something that is similar to something else.²⁶² MacArthur and Mayhue state that it conveys the idea of something that is a "copy" of an original.²⁶³ In 1 Sam 6:5, image (צֶלֶם) is used to describe the tumors and mice made as gifts by the Philistines when they returned the Ark of the Covenant to the Israelites. The word is also used in Amos 5:16 to describe the idols of heathen gods.

If the intent of צֶלֶם is to describe a copy of an original, the question must be asked "How is man similar to, or a copy of, YHWH?" This has stimulated much discussion among theologians through the ages. MacArthur and Mayhue identify three broad categories to describe the image of God in man: (1) the substantive view, where the image of God is structurally inherent in man; (2) the functional view, where the image of God in man is a reference to actions man is able to perform; and (3) the relational view, where the image of God describes the ability to interact intelligently with others.²⁶⁴ All three can be plausibly incorporated into the understanding of צֶלֶם. However, the substantive view is to be preferred because the functional and the relational are consequences of the structural.²⁶⁵ Furthermore, the structural view best reflects the meaning of the צֶלֶם, which describes some similarity or copy of what is found in the character of God.

What is that similarity or copy of God in man? Suggestions include man's intellectual ability; man's moral capabilities; man's original moral perfection; and man's power over God's creation.²⁶⁶

---

²⁶² Grudem, *Systematic Theology*, 442, fn. 7.

²⁶³ MacArthur and Mayhue, *Biblical Doctrine*, 410. MacArthur and Mayhue present a helpful illustration to understand this Hebrew word by noting that in the ancient world rulers would display an image of themselves to symbolize their sovereignty in the area they ruled. Thus, man as the image-bearer of God represents God as vice-regent or mediator over God's creation.

²⁶⁴ MacArthur and Mayhue, *Biblical Doctrine*, 412–413.

²⁶⁵Ibid., 413.

²⁶⁶ Grudem, *Systematic Theology*, 443.

This understanding of צֶלֶם is not found in Eastern Orthodoxy, as we shall see shortly.

But what does it mean to be created in the likeness of God? The word likeness (דְמוּת) is a comparative term used to describe something that resembles something else.[267] It describes something that is similar but not exactly like something else in reality.[268] In Ezek 1:5, there were figures resembling living beings that had human form—they looked human, but they were not human. They had the likeness of a man but they were not men. Once again, this understanding of דְמוּת cannot be found in Eastern Orthodox thinking, as we shall see shortly.

Both צֶלֶם and דְמוּת convey the concept of similarity to the original.[269] Both words imply there are also dissimilarities between the original and the copy. The use of these two different words with similar meanings indicate a synonymous relationship between them. As a result, it would be safe to agree with Grudem when he says that Gen 1:26 conveys the purpose for being created in the image and likeness of God. This verse describes man being created like God (although with severe limitations) in order to represent God among the rest of creation.[270]

Conversely, Eastern Orthodoxy uses צֶלֶם (tselem) to describe humanity's free will, endowed by God, that possesses the ability to know God.[271] In other words, to be created in the image of God means

---

[267] *NIDOTTE,* "דמת," 1:967.

[268] *BDB,* דְמוּת, 1823.

[269] *NIDOTTE,* "Form, Image" 4:644.

[270] Grudem, *Systematic Theology,* 443.

[271] Ware, *The Orthodox Church,* 219. Bishop Kallistos, with the blessing of Eastern Orthodox theologians, quotes John of Damascus as saying, "The expression according to the image indicates rationality and freedom." Bishop Kallistos understands this quote to describe how humans are separate from animals, Bishop Kallistos posits that man has free will, rationality, and a sense of moral responsibility. While not lexically true, this is conceptually true. But should this understanding be philosophically imposed upon the word or the context of Gen 1:26 and Gen 5:3?

to be created with an internal sense of moral responsibility to seek out the knowledge of and relationship with the Creator. More simply expressed, Eastern Orthodoxy's understanding of man's image is that it is the propensity or desire within man to know God personally. Additionally, the Eastern Orthodox concept of the image of God is the speculation that its creation in man was initially incomplete. By their own admission, their view of God's creation of man is less exalted than the Western Church's understanding.[272] The Western Church (both Roman Catholic and Protestant) teaches a completeness in man's creation. According to Eastern Orthodoxy, man was not created perfect; instead, he was created with a need and desire to complete a process leading to perfection.[273] Where do the Eastern Orthodox get this idea? From their philosophical definitions of image and likeness.

The term likeness (דְּמוּת) also is interpreted philosophically within Eastern Orthodox theology. For them, the term describes the work necessary to accomplish the goal of knowing and being united with God. Likeness means to "assimilate" to God through virtuous effort.[274] Stated differently, Eastern Orthodoxy defines *image* as the desire to know God, and *likeness* as the accomplishment of knowing God after great personal effort. Humanity cannot lose the image of God, but the likeness of God can only be acquired through man's personal effort. This likeness is acquired by making moral choices with assistance from God by His grace (i.e., His energies).[275]

With such understandings of image and likeness to describe

---

[272] Ibid., 223.

[273] Mantzaridis, *The Deification of Man*, 124.

[274] Ware, *The Orthodox Church*, 219. In the same paragraph, Ware quotes John of Damascus by saying "the expression according to the likeness indicates assimilation to God through virtue." As is true of the Eastern Orthodox understanding of *the image of God*, this is not lexically true but more dramatically it is a philosophical imposition upon not only the word but the contexts of Gen 1:26 and Gen 5:3.

[275] Ibid.

humanity's relationship to God, it is not surprising that forensic justification is an alien concept in Eastern Orthodoxy. The God-centered message of the gospel is replaced with a man-centered focus that emphasizes human effort.

How did the Eastern Orthodox arrive at these definitions of image and likeness? It most certainly was not from a linguistic study of either the Hebrew Scriptures or the LXX, since the Hebrew and Greek meanings of these words possess a different meaning than found within Eastern Orthodoxy. In fact, Eastern Orthodox discussions on man being created in the image and likeness of God typically begin philosophically, not biblically or lexically. For example, in his book *Orthodox Theology,* Vladimir Lossky begins his discussion on *image* and *likeness* by saying, "Ancient philosophy understood the central condition of man and expressed it through the nature of the 'microcosm.'"[276] He then uses five paragraphs to philosophize about the nature of humanity before introducing a non-lexical understanding of the image of God in humanity. He writes, "The image, then, cannot be objectified, 'naturalized' we might say, by being attributed to some part or other of the human being."[277] He is making it clear that the foundation of his understanding of God's image in man has a Greek, philosophical foundation and not a lexical one.

Bishop Kallistos does the same thing. In his discussion of image and likeness. he uses a philosophical approach to define the terms. His authorities are the philosophical thoughts of the Greek Fathers rather than a lexical understanding of the canon. Bishop Kallistos states, "According to most of the Greek Fathers, the terms image and likeness do not mean the same thing."[278] He then develops an understanding of these terms by beginning with a quote from John of Damascus: "The expression according to the image indicates

---

[276] Vladimir Lossky, *Orthodox Theology* (Crestwood, NY: St. Vladimir's Seminary Press, 1978), 70.

[277] Lossky., 71.

[278] Ware, *The Orthodox Church*, 219.

rationality and freedom, while the expression according to the likeness indicates assimilation to God through virtue."[279] While John of Damascus' understanding of image resembles the conclusion of the substantive view in Reformed thinking stated above, his conclusion is not achieved through a lexical approach, but philosophically. More importantly, it is combined with a non-biblical, philosophical, man-centered understanding of likeness. Rather than being a synonymous term with image, Bishop Kallistos concludes with John of Damascus that it describes an end result after the exertion of significant effort.

John Anthony McGuckin openly admits the philosophical starting point of the Eastern Orthodox understanding of *image* and *likeness*. He admits Eastern Orthodoxy borrows heavily from Aristotle's categories and "actually reverses the methodological principles of Hellenism" in their attempt to understand human nature. [280] Here he notes that the Eastern Orthodox understanding of man is based on a Greek philosophical approach rather than a biblical foundation.

Mantzaridis, however, comes the closest to interacting lexically with the terms "image" and "likeness" by relying on the Greek texts, though omitting consideration of the Hebrew Scriptures, to understand the words. He cites a source that says the LXX's use of likeness "expresses something dynamic and not yet realized, whereas the word image signifies a realized state, which in the present context constitutes the starting point for the attainment of the likeness."[281] His concept of image and likeness is thoroughly Eastern Orthodox in thinking as evidenced by describing image as common to all men but likeness as an unrealized potential or goal for man.[282] While acknowledging that modern commentators (Mantzardis' way of describing Reformed thinkers) understand the Hebrew terms as synonymous, he nonetheless insists that the terms are distinct by using

---

[279] Ibid.

[280] John Anthony McGuckin, *The Orthodox Church* (Malden, MA: Blackwell Publishing, 2008), 187.

[281] Mantzaridis, *The Deification of Man*, 21.

[282] Mantzaridis., 21–22.

the LXX as his defense.[283]

It should be evident by now that there is no lexical evidence to support the claim that צֶלֶם (tselem) and דְּמוּת (d'muth) describe "a propensity to know" and "the accomplishment of a goal after great effort." Rather, they are used synonymously to describe, in an emphatic way, that humanity is created by God with moral attributes similar to His own (cf. Col 3:10).[284]

As a result, Eastern Orthodox redefinitions of image and likeness present a different picture and a different understanding of humanity's creation and fall than described in the biblical narrative. From the Eastern Orthodox perspective, Adam and Eve were not created knowing God because they were not created perfect. Instead, they were created with the desire to be perfect and the desire to pursue perfection as well as the knowledge of God through their own personal efforts.

From an Eastern Orthodox perspective, Adam and Eve were created with a propensity to know and seek after God. And after significant effort on their part, they could have accomplished their goal of knowing and uniting with Him had it not been for their disobedience to God when they ate the forbidden fruit. They "fell off the path" in their pursuit to be one with God and they cannot get back on the path without help or assistance. Assistance for them and their offspring comes in the form of Christ's work on the cross, which enables them to continue their effort to be united with God. In the words of Bishop Kallistos, "Endowed with the image from the start, they were called to acquire the likeness by their own efforts (assisted of course by the grace of God)."[285]

---

[283] Mantzaridis., 21.

[284] George Bush, *Notes on Genesis*, 2 vol. (Minneapolis: James & Klock Publishing, 1979), 1:41.

[285] Ware, *The Orthodox Church*, 219.

# The Effect of Misunderstanding Justification, Grace and of Being Created in the Image and Likeness of God on the Biblical Understanding of Faith

This understanding of צֶלֶם (tselem) and דְּמוּת (d'muth) has also negatively impacted the Eastern Orthodox understanding of "faith" (πίστις). While translated as "trust," "faith," "assurance," or "belief," the term is embedded with the concept of "confidence" or "certainty" or "conviction." When a person confesses that faith saves, what is he saying? In general, he should be declaring that he has confidence in the object of his faith. He is certain that the object of his faith will rescue (save) him from the acute danger that is facing him in eternity. But what is the object of his faith?

For Eastern Orthodoxy, the object of faith or confidence is in a process known as deification. Within Eastern Orthodoxy, being created in the "image" of God means that man was created imperfect with the desire to be perfect like God.[286] But man was also created in the "likeness" of God. By the Eastern Orthodox definition, this means a person has the ability to acquire the perfection necessary through a synergistic effort with God.[287] According to the Eastern Orthodox, then, Adam and Eve were on the path to knowing God fully through deification. Sin, however, caused them to fall off the path, and without divine help to get back on the path they were heading to eternal damnation.[288] However, in the fullness of the time, God sent forth His Son, born of a woman and under the Law, to do a work that would make it possible for humanity to get back on the path and resume their process for obtaining the likeness of God through great effort.[289]

The Eastern Orthodox call this process deification (θέωσις). This manufactured term by the Eastern Orthodox summarizes in one term what the Bible and Reformed Protestants use three terms to

---

[286] Ibid.

[287] Ware, *The Orthodox Church*, 219, 223.

[288] Ware, Timothy, *The Orthodox Church.*, 220.

[289] Ware, Timothy., 225.

describe—salvation, justification, and sanctification.[290] Eastern Orthodoxy goes on to argue that deification begins in this life and continues into eternity until the likeness of God is fully realized.[291] This process involves the help of God, Mary,[292] and the saints,[293] who dispense grace (known as the energies of God) to the one who seeks their help or assistance. Therefore, to the Eastern Orthodox, their faith is the process of making one righteous and holy (justified and sanctified) in order to be deified (fully saved).[294] Thus, the confidence of the Eastern Orthodox follower is in an eternal process, or, a conviction that his persevering efforts to obtain or acquire the grace (the energies) of God will result in knowing God (being fully accepted by God). Similar to Gal 1:8–9, Paul would anathematize this so-called gospel because their confidence is found in a process of being made righteous (becoming justified and becoming sanctified) rather than in the completeness and sufficiency of Christ's work on the cross, which results in being "declared righteous" by faith alone.

Some Slavic Protestantsts, having lived under the influence of Eastern Orthodox thinking, face the same anathema in Gal 1:8–9. Like Eastern Orthodoxy, some Slavic Protestantsts view Jesus' atoning work as making salvation possible through his or her self-determination to be made righteous (justified) and holy (sanctified). Christ's righteousness is acquired by effort, not declared, conferred, or imputed by faith alone. The primary difference between some Slavic Protestants and Eastern Orthodoxy is the terminus of the effort. Some Slavic Protestants understand the process of deification culminating at physical death (Heb 9:27) whereas the Eastern Orthodox Church believes the process continues into eternity until it is fully realized.

---

[290] Fairbairn, *Eastern Orthodoxy through Western Eyes*, 122.

[291] Fairbairn, Donald., 91–92.

[292] Fairbairn, Donald., 102.

[293] Fairbairn, Donald., 99.

[294] Ware, *The Orthodox Church,* 231–38.

This concept that "faith alone is not enough" has remained with both the Roman Catholic Church and the Eastern Orthodox Church for centuries. Proof can be seen in more modern Eastern Orthodox authors. One such author is Georges Florovsky (1893-1979) who wrote *The Byzantine Ascetic and Spiritual Fathers*: "For Luther 'to justify'—δικαιουν—meant to declare righteous or just, not 'to make' righteous or just—it is an appeal to an extrinsic justice which in reality is spiritual fiction."[295] Furthermore, the explanation of Acts 10:35 in *The Orthodox Study Bible* says,

> Justification is not merely a one-time event, but a dynamic, ongoing process. In addition to faith, two conditions are given here: God accepts whoever fears Him and works righteousness. This does not deny justification by faith but demonstrates clearly that justification is not by faith alone (Jas 2:24).[296]

Before all these thoughts can be tied together, one must also reexamine the Eastern Orthodox understanding of δικαιόω (justification). Jerome in the West and John of Damascus in the East were great ecclesiastical influencers from the 4th century onward. As mentioned previously, Jerome translated the Greek word δικαιόω into the Latin Vulgate using the word *iustificare*. This altered the biblical meaning of justification from "being declared righteous" to "being made righteous." It transferred the concept from the forensic realm into the theoretical. John of Damascus, building on this Latin concept, developed it further by redefining "likeness" as the accomplishment of knowing God after great personal effort. And Cyril of Alexandria contributed to this ecclesiastical confusion by fusing justification and sanctification into synonymous terms.

In response to Florovsky, a careful examination of Scripture will show that it was not Luther who introduced this definition and

---

[295] Georges Florovsky's, *Collected Works*, vol. 10: *The Byzantine Ascetic and Spiritual Fathers*, trans. Raymond Miller et al. (Vaduz, Germany: Büchervertriebsanstalt, 1987), 31.

[296] *The Orthodox Study Bible* (Nashville: Thomas Nelson Publishers, 2009), 1487.

understanding of justification, but the Holy Spirit specifically using the δικαιόω word group in Paul's writings to the Romans and the Galatians. The necessity of forensic justification is exactly what God wanted to communicate to His fallen creation and Paul, through his ministry and the canonical writings that have been passed down through the Church for centuries, forcefully communicated this message.

In response to those asserting a non-forensic, non-monergistic justification through faith plus effort, it is noteworthy to see Paul's argument in Gal 2:16—Paul's first preserved writing. In his defense of the gospel of grace to the Galatians, who were beginning to abandon their faith-based salvation for a works-based salvation, Paul used a living example to defend his understanding of forensic justification. He did this in response to Peter's own error, which makes his living example all the more powerful.

In Galatians 2, Peter—the leader of the apostles appointed by Jesus—is rebuked by Paul— a younger convert. Paul admonishes Peter against abandoning his faith-based justification for a works-based justification. In Gal 2:16, Paul emphatically proclaims: "We have believed in Christ Jesus, that we may be justified by faith in Christ, and not by works of the law, since by works of the Law shall no flesh be justified." Paul strongly asserts that confidence (faith) in the divine, forensic declaration of righteousness results in salvation; there is no hint of confidence in his own efforts!

So, when the Eastern Orthodox Church develops its understanding of image and likeness, combined with its definition of grace and justification, it produces a damning gospel message (cf., Gal 1:9–10). Its gospel describes a process of man-centered religious effort but not salvation itself. The most dangerous question to ask in a Slavic culture is "Are you saved by grace *alone*?," because they can legitimately answer (from their perspective) "Yes, I am saved by grace alone!" But what they mean is, "I am in the process of obtaining salvation by trying to accumulate enough grace in order to be fully united with God sometime in eternity."

Regrettably, in my twenty-five years of ministry among the Slavic people, I have found some Slavic Protestants all too often expressing this Eastern Orthodox concept of justification and the role of grace. Some Slavic Protestants will repudiate the Eastern Orthodox religion in word but not in actual worldview. Their concept of justification remains influenced by the Slavic culture in which they live. Why is this true?

Sergiy Tarasenko makes an accurate assessment in his examination of the historical and doctrinal influences of Eastern Orthodox theology on some Slavic Baptists. He sees the lack of indigenous, published systematic theologies as a reason for the different perspective on justification by grace through faith.[297]

---

[297] Sergiy S. Tarasenko, "The Historical And Doctrinal Influences of the Russian Orthodox Church on the Soteriology of the Russian Baptists," 13.

# CHAPTER EIGHT

## THE EFFECT OF RE-DEFINING JUSITIFICATION ON THE CONCEPT OF FAITH
### Faith

One of the obstacles for the teacher and preacher of God's Word is the use of clichés—words that are used repeatedly to summarize a concept with the assumption that the audience understands that word's full meaning. Over time the meaning and concept behind the cliché can become lost and then redefined. In other cases, it can become so generally defined that the concept embedded in the Greek word is somewhat neutralized. "Faith" has become a Christian cliché whose meaning is assumed in Roman Catholic, Eastern Orthodox and Protestant usage but either not carefully or correctly defined.

Grudem gives a summary definition of faith as, "Trust or dependence on God based on the fact that we take him at his word and believe what he said."[298] While this is a good general definition there are shades of the Greek term that can further enhance our understanding of the word. The noun "faith" (πίστις, *pistis*) and its verbal form "I believe" (πιστεύω, *pisteuō*) are variously translated in English Bibles as "trust," "faith," "assurance," and "belief." All have elements of accuracy when being translated in the English Bible. In fact, Grudem emphasizes the word "trust" in his understanding of "faith."[299] However, there is a concept associated with the word that is often overlooked: "confidence," "certainty," and "conviction."[300] Berkhof captures this concept of "confidence" in his definition of "faith." He says that πίστις has two meanings: it is a "conviction based upon confidence in a person" and "the confidence itself on which the

---

[298] Grudem, *Systematic Theology*, 1242.

[299] Grudem., 710.

[300] *TDNT*, "πίστις," 3:175–76

conviction rests."³⁰¹ As a result, another way to describe faith is confidence in an object that can be relied upon, or facts about an object upon which you can place your trust. This is supported by *NIDTTE* when it notes that early usage of "faith" (πίστις) by Homer had the sense of "worthy of trust ... credible."³⁰²

Faith is comprised of three elements: *notitia* (knowledge), *assensus* (assent) and *fiducia* (trust).³⁰³ *Notitia* is information that is acknowledged as fact by someone, *assensus* is information that is acknowledged as true, and *fiducia* is knowledge that is acknowledged as true fact and has been personally embraced as true.

As it relates to the gospel, *notitia* knowledge is acknowledging that Jesus lived, claimed He was God in flesh, died in man's place to take man's deserved wrath from God for personal sin, and rose again on the third day as He promised to do. These basic elements of the gospel are contained in Matthew 16:13-23 where in answer to Jesus' question to the disciples, He is acknowledged as God (16:16, 17) who came in the flesh (16:13-15) for the purpose of redeeming sinners (16:21-23). All this is predicated—as MacArthur has noted—on acknowledging God's holiness, man's sinfulness, Christ's identity and Christ's accomplishment on the cross.³⁰⁴ Of immense importance is the acknowledgement of Jesus' resurrection (1 Corinthians 15:3, 4). For the gospel to do its transforming work, these basic facts must be presented and acknowledged. If these facts are not acknowledged as facts, there will be no progress toward assensus which must culminate in fiducia for salvation to be accomplished.

*Assensus* knowledge is accepting notitia facts as true. It was at this stage of faith that Jesus lost many of His followers. In John 6:22-66, Jesus described Himself as the Bread of Life. After great explanation, Jesus called for a conclusion to be made about His claims. In verse 66 a conclusion was made and many of His disciples

---

[301] Berkhof, *Systematic Theology*, 494.

[302] *NIDNTTE,* "πιστεύω," 3:759.

[303] MacArthur and Mayhue, *Biblical Doctrine*, 596.

[304] Ibid, 597..

withdrew and stopped walking with Him—they ceased to be His followers because they refused—at that time—to accept the facts He presented about Himself as true!

But *fiducia* knowledge is embracing and putting confidence in assensus facts and expressing this confidence by becoming a follower (cf. Matt 16:24-26).[305] We see fiducia in Hebrews 11:1; Philippians 3:4-7, John 1:12 and 2 Timothy 1:12. There is an eager pursuit of accepting the gospel facts as true and becoming a joyful follower of Jesus that seeks to conform one's life to His teaching for God's glory out of gratitude for the gift of salvation given through faith alone.

How does this understanding of faith relate to this biblical orthodoxy? Is *notitia* faith a confident reliance upon the monergistic work of Jesus, or is it synergistic with an emphasis of confidence and reliance on the work of a believer? The Eastern Orthodox promote a synergistic faith emphasizing the work of man. This way of thinking is often similarly embraced by the Slavic Baptist community. One of the goals of this book is to demonstrate that true, biblical salvation is confidence (faith) in the monergistic work of God resulting in a present, forensic justification that promises a complete spiritual transformation at physical death merely by gazing at the face of Jesus, the object of our faith (1 John 3:2).

---

[305] John MacArthur and Richard Mayhue., 598. MacArthur and Mayhue insightfully quote Murray, who said, "Faith is knowledge passing into conviction, and it is conviction passing into confidence" (see John Murray, *Redemption Accomplished and Applied* [Grand Rapids: Eerdmans, 2015], 117).

# CHAPTER NINE

## THE EFFECT OF RE-DEFINING JUSITIFICATION ON THE CONCEPT OF SANCTIFICATION

### Sanctification

Although sanctification is an element of salvation, it is often identified as synonymous with salvation. "Being saved" is often conceptually associated with "being sanctified," which in turn is often associated with "being made presentable to enter into God's eternal presence."

Like salvation, sanctification is used to describe three different time elements of the believer's confidence in the work of the cross of Jesus Christ.[306] It can be used to describe the initial, monergistic work of God in the believer's past and specifically termed "positional" or "definitive" sanctification (see Acts 20:32; 1 Cor 1:2; 6:11; Heb 10:10).[307] Grudem notes that this "initial moral change is the first stage in sanctification."[308] Berkhof describes this initial regenerative work of God as "that gracious and continuous operation of the Holy Spirit, by which He delivers the justified sinner from the pollution of sin, renews the whole nature in the image of God, and enables him to perform good works."[309] This monergistic work of God places the justified sinner in an acceptable position with God in preparation for God's final sanctifying work.

While positional or definitive sanctification is the manifestation of justification that frees the justified sinner from the power of sin,[310] there is an on-going transformation of the justified

---

[306] MacArthur and Mayhue, *Biblical Doctrine*, 936.

[307] John MacArthur and Richard Mayhue., 364.

[308] Grudem, *Systematic Theology*, 747.

[309] Berkhof, *Systematic Theology*, 532.

[310] MacArthur and Mayhue, *Biblical Doctrine,* 633.

sinner that is known as "progressive sanctification."[311] This is a synergistic work of God in the lives of believers after conversion (see 1 Thess 4:4; 2 Cor 3:18; 7:1). Berkhof calls this a cooperation of the justified sinner with God.[312] Grudem reminds us that this cooperative effort increases within the justified sinner throughout life.[313] Herman Bavinck wisely notes that "Those who are born of God increasingly become the children of God and bear his image and likeness, because in principle they already are his children. The rule of organic life applies to them: Become what you are!"[314] It should be noted that when Bavinck describes one who is born of God as "becoming the children of God," he is saying that in light of the definitions of justification, sanctification and salvation, that believers are "*demonstrating* themselves to be what they profess to be."

There is also a final and future monergistic, sanctifying work of God upon man known as "perfected sanctification" or "glorification" (see 2 Thess 2:13; Phil 1:6; 1 John 3:2).[315] Berkhof notes that this must "be completed either at the very moment of death, or immediately after death, as far as the soul is concerned, and at the resurrection in so far as it pertains to the body."[316] This culmination of salvation is achieved when the Lord resurrects our bodies.[317]

In 1 John 3:2–3 the Apostle John identifies all three time components associated with sanctification. He says, "Beloved, now we are children of God [positional sanctification], and it has not appeared as yet what we shall be [progressive sanctification]. We

---

[311] John MacArthur and Richard Mayhue., 635.

[312] Berkhof, *Systematic Theology*, 534.

[313] Grudem, *Systematic Theology*, 748.

[314] Herman Bavinck, *Reformed Dogmatics*, 4 vols. (Grand Rapids: Baker, 2001), 4:255.

[315] MacArthur and Mayhue, *Biblical Doctrine*, 365.

[316] Berkhof, *Systematic Theology*, 534.

[317] Grudem, *Systematic Theology*, 749.

know that when He appears, we shall be like Him, because we shall see Him just as He is [perfected sanctification or glorification]."

In the words of MacArthur and Mayhue, both salvation and sanctification describe the "inauguration, continuation, or culmination in the context of redemption," and unless one is willing to accept this tension of distinctions with the terms, serious errors will develop in the understanding of God's working within man.[318] This is the understanding of sanctification that is being utilized in this book.

Eastern Orthodoxy, however, does not use the biblical term "sanctification" but rather describes this activity as "deification" (*theosis*). What does Eastern Orthodoxy mean by "deification"? While the definition of the term is relatively easy to understand, the concept behind the term is not easy for Protestants to grasp. It is not easy because it is not a biblical term. It is not used by any New Testament writer. Therefore, it is a philosophically rather than a lexically derived term. It is best summarized by redefining and combining together into one word (that is, "deification" or θέωσις) the general understanding of the biblical terms' salvation, sanctification, and justification.[319] While the lexical study of salvation, sanctification, and justification reveal sharp distinctions in meaning between these words, Eastern Orthodoxy does not acknowledge these lexical distinctions. Instead, Eastern Orthodoxy in defining "deification," prefers to make a sharp distinction between the "essence" of God and the "energies" of God when discussing "deification."[320] Why does Eastern Orthodoxy prefer to focus on the distinctions between God's "essence" and God's "energies"? It is the result of misunderstanding the phrase "that through these you may become partakers of the divine nature" (OSB) found in 2 Peter 1:4.

---

[318] MacArthur and Mayhue, *Biblical Doctrine*, 361.

[319] Clendenin, *Eastern Orthodox Christianity*, 159. Clendenin in his evaluation of deification notes that Eastern Orthodoxy does not make a distinction between salvation and sanctification but confuses the two with an emphasis on sanctification.

[320] Ware, Timothy, *The Orthodox Church*, 232.

Deification, according to Eastern Orthodoxy, simply means "the process by which a Christian becomes more like God."[321] Eastern Orthodoxy begins by building their understanding of deification based upon statements made by early church fathers such as Athanasius.[322] Athanasius (d. 373 AD) is quoted as saying "God became human that we might be made god."[323] Much earlier, Irenaeus (130–202 AD) had said "If the Word is made man, it is that men might become gods."[324] Basil the Great (330–379 AD), a contemporary of Athanasius, said "From the Holy Spirit there is the likeness of God, and the highest of all things to be desired, to become God."[325] It is upon these statements by Athanasius, Irenaeus and Basil the Great that Eastern Orthodoxy begins to philosophically interpret 2 Peter 1:4 in building the concept of deification.

Though Eastern Orthodoxy philosophically interprets 2 Peter 1:4, they nonetheless claim that deification is a literal[326] and constant theme in John's Gospel and the writings of Paul.[327] While the *Orthodox Study Bible* asserts that John 10:34–36 supports the concept of deification, the footnote directs the reader to 2 Peter 1:4 as the proof text for this understanding. But this reasoning is circular since the explanation of 2 Peter 1:4 makes a reference back to John 10:34–36.[328] A full page in *The Orthodox Study Bible* is devoted to explaining how 2 Peter 1:4 describes deification, but it is also the only place in *The*

---

[321] St. Athanasius Academy of Orthodox Theology, *The Orthodox Study Bible,* 1692.

[322] Ware, Timothy, *The Orthodox Church*, 21, 231-232.

[323] Ibid., 21.

[324] Clendenin, *Eastern Orthodox Christianity*.

[325] Ibid. 117.

[326] Ware, Timothy, *The Orthodox Church,* 21.

[327] Ibid., 231.

[328] St. Athanasius Academy of Orthodox Theology, *The Orthodox Study Bible*.

*Orthodox Study Bible* devoted to its explanation.[329]

How does Eastern Orthodoxy arrive at the conclusion that the phrase in 2 Peter 1:4 ("that through these you may become partakers of the divine nature") is the proof text for deification? While they correctly state that "becoming partakers of the divine nature" cannot mean humans becoming divine because humans cannot take on the nature or essences of God,[330] they then invent the idea that Peter is describing the union of humans with the divine nature through divine energies.[331] This idea does not come from the biblical text. Instead, they use philosophy and a re-definition of the word θεὸς to arrive at the conclusion that Peter is describing union with the energies of God.[332]

How do the Eastern Orthodox propose that the "energies" of God deify their adherents? While they rightly answer, "by grace,"[333] what they mean is completely foreign to the teaching of God's word. While Eph 2:8–9 teaches that grace is a divine, monergistic gift through a divinely provided faith, the Eastern Orthodox, on the other

---

[329] Ibid., 1692.

[330] Ibid.

[331] Ware, Timothy, *The Orthodox Church,* 231.

[332] St. Athanasius Academy of Orthodox Theology, *The Orthodox Study Bible*. The Eastern Orthodox redefine θεὸς using the following logic. Citing an observation made by John of Damascus, they state "The word "God" in the Scriptures refers not to the divine nature or essence, for that is unknowable. "God" refers to the divine energies—the power and grace of God that we can perceive in this world. The Greek word for God, *theos*, comes from a verb meaning "run," "see," or "burn." These are energy words, so to speak. Not essence words." But contrary to the observation attributed to John of Damascus, there is absolutely no etymological justification for such an Eastern Orthodox redefinition of θεὸς. Stauffer in *TDNT* begins his discussion of θεὸς by saying "The question of the etym. of θεὸς has never been solved. It can thus tell us nothing about the nature of the Gk. concept of God." (*TDNT*, 3:67). Furthermore, he goes on to state that θεὸς was increasingly used to describe metaphysical powers and forces (*TDNT*, 3:69), not actions of "running", "seeing," or "burning" as the Eastern Orthodox claim. Finally, Stauffer states that the Greek concept is determined by Homer's use of the word which is used in an ethical sense (*TDNT*, 3:71).

[333] Ware, Timothy, *The Orthodox Church,* 68.

hand, teach that "Grace is God's uncreated *ENERGY* bestowed in the sacraments and is therefore truly experienced."[334] According to Eastern Orthodoxy, grace is acquired when adherents to Eastern Orthodoxy participate in church ordained activities. Thus, grace is acquired through faith (confidence) in one's participatory efforts in the process of deification[335] rather than faith (confidence) alone in the finished work of Christ on the cross. It is a process that does not end in this life but continues until the Last Day.[336]

While Eastern Orthodoxy can rightly describe what we call progressive sanctification as a synergistic activity (see Phil 2:12), its emphasis incorrectly makes it a synergistic work between God and man in the whole of salvation, placing a dominant focus upon man's contribution. Ware is noticeably clear on Eastern Orthodoxy's synergistic salvation and sanctification. He writes,

> The Orthodox Church rejects any doctrine of grace which might seem to infringe upon human freedom. To describe the relation between the grace of God and human freedom, Orthodoxy uses the term co-operation or synergy (synergia); in Paul's words: "We are fellow workers (synergoi) with God" (1 Corinthians iii, 9). If we are to achieve full fellowship with God, we cannot do so without God's help, yet we must also play our own part; we humans as well as God must make our contribution to the common work, although what God does is of immeasurably greater importance than what we do. "The incorporation of humans into Christ and our union with God require the co-operation of two unequal, but equally necessary forces: divine grace and human will." The supreme example of synergy is

---

[334] St. Athanasius Academy of Orthodox Theology, *The Orthodox Study Bible*. See also Ware, *The Orthodox Church*, 68.

[335] Ware, Timothy, *The Orthodox Church*, 236.

[336] Ibid., 235-236. See also OSB, 1692.

the Mother of God.³³⁷

Ultimately, "deification" as a theological term is not found in the Bible; it is a contrivance in Eastern Orthodox thinking. The words used in the NT to describe sanctification and a related word translated "holy" are ἅγιος (*hagios*), ἁγιάζω (*hagiazō*), and ἁγιασμός (*hagiasmos*). The most basic understanding of the word group is "to bring into a close relationship."³³⁸ Vine describes this activity in the NT as either a "separation to" God (Acts 20:32; Rom 15:16) or a "separation from" evil or the world (John 17:17, 19).³³⁹ *NIDNTTE* adds that the word group has the understanding of "to stand in awe of, respect, dread."³⁴⁰ What is woefully apparent in the concept of deification is that Eastern Orthodoxy has abandoned the lexical meanings of salvation, sanctification, and justification substituting in their place a non-biblical word, deification, that has a philosophically derived meaning producing anathematized concepts of these key biblical terms relating to salvation.

---

³³⁷ Ibid., 221–22. You will notice that Ware includes two quotations in his statement. The first is traced to a Monk of the Eastern Church and quoted from page 23 of a book entitled *Orthodox Spirituality*. The second is a comment Ware makes later in his book on page 258: "Among all God's creatures, she [Mary] is the supreme example of synergy or co-operation between the purpose of deity and human freedom. God, who always respects our liberty of choice, did not wish to become incarnate without the willing consent of His Mother. He waited for her voluntary response." In a continuation of his thought, he quotes Nicolas Cabasilas, who said "The Incarnation was not only the work of the Father, of His power and His Spirit . . . but it was also the work of the will and faith of the Virgin. . . . Just as God became Incarnate voluntarily, so He wished that His Mother should bear Him freely and with her full consent."

³³⁸ *TDNT*, "ἅγιος," 1:12.

³³⁹ *EDNTW*, "Sanctification," 3:317.

³⁴⁰ *NIDNTTE,* "ἅγιος," 1:124.

# CHAPTER TEN

# THE THEOLOGICAL HISTORY OF THE CHURCH AND THE SLAVIC PROTESTANTS

## Eastern Orthodox History

The church of Jesus Christ began in the eastern part of the Mediterranean world at Jerusalem on the day of Pentecost around AD 30 (see Acts 2). From there Scripture attests that the next named church was also located in the eastern part of the Mediterranean world, in the city of Antioch (Acts 11:19). Over time, churches were developed in the two major metropolitan centers of the Roman world. In the east was Alexandria, which contained a population of one million by the first century.[341] The city was developed as a Greek cultural training center by Alexander the Great in 332 B.C. At a crossroads between the east and the west, it developed not only as a commercial center but additionally as an educational center influenced by a renowned library that attracted scholars from around the world.[342] It was from Alexandria that Hellenist Jews translated the Hebrew Scriptures into Greek in what came to be known as the Septuagint.[343] It was in Alexandria that a Christian training center was later developed that included the likes of Clement of Alexandria and Origen.[344]

In the west was Rome, the capital of the Roman Empire, the location of a church to which Paul wrote, and the traditional site of

---

[341] E. M. Blaiklock, "Alexandria," in *Zondervan Pictorial Encyclopedia of the Bible*, 4 vols, ed. Merrill C. Tenney(Grand Rapids: Zondervan, 1975), 1:102.

[342] Prudence J. Jones, "Alexandria," in *The Oxford Encyclopedia of Ancient Greece and Rome*, ed. Michael Garagin (Oxford: Oxford, 2010), 71.

[343] E. M. Blaiklock, "Alexandria," 1:101.

[344] Williston Walker, *A History of the Christian Church* (New York: Scribners, 1970), 72–77.

martyrdom for Peter and Paul. As the church expanded, new churches came under the regional control of the regional center (i.e., Rome, Alexandria, Antioch, and Jerusalem) closest to them. On November 8, 324 A.D., the Roman emperor Constantine began construction of a new capital for the Roman Empire, which took almost six years to complete.[345] On May 11, 330, he moved the capital of the empire to Constantinople (modern day Istanbul).[346] Because of the city's economic, political, and religious significance in the empire, it was given regional authority at the second church council (Constantinople I) in 381 A.D. and enjoyed a religious influence second only to Rome.[347]

Together, these churches were known as catholic and orthodox. "Catholic", a term first used by Ignatius to describe the church in the Platonic sense of its "universal" influence,[348] and "orthodox" to describe the church as having the "right belief" and the "right worship" of God.[349] The sharp distinction between the Eastern churches and the Western churches came at the Great Schism in 1054 A.D., when the Western churches took the title Roman Catholic while the Eastern churches took the term Eastern Orthodox ("Eastern" because they were in the eastern part of the Roman Empire). The term Orthodox, as self-defined by those designated in this way, means that "they regard their Church as the Church which guards and teaches the true belief about God and which glorifies Him with right worship, that

---

[345] Mehmet Fatih Yavuz, "Byzantium," in *The Oxford Encyclopedia of Ancient Greece and Rome*, 1:36.

[346] Ware, *The Orthodox Church*, 18, 19. Ware says Constantine's motive for moving the capital from Rome to Constantinople was religious. From Constantine's perspective, Rome was "too deeply stained with pagan associations" to be the religious capital of the empire.

[347] Ware, Timothy., 23. The early church recognized a descending order of influence beginning with Rome, then Constantinople, Alexandria, Antioch, and Jerusalem even though they viewed themselves as equal among equals.

[348] Walker, *A History of the Christian Church*, 57.

[349] Ware, *The Orthodox Church*, 8.

is, *as nothing less than the Church of Christ on earth.*"³⁵⁰

The Eastern Orthodox Church organizes itself around four ancient Patriarchates, nine autocephalous churches, and several autonomous churches. A Patriarchal church is one of the original, historical regional church centers (Constantinople, Alexandria, Antioch, and Jerusalem). An autocephalous church is one that was been granted independent authority by one of the patriarchal churches in the past (Russia, Serbia, Romania, Bulgaria, Georgia, Cyprus, Greece, Poland, and Albania).³⁵¹ An autonomous church is self-governing but not possessing full independence from a patriarchal or autocephalous church. Examples of autonomous churches include the Orthodox Church of the Czech Lands and Slovakia, Sinai, Finland, Japan, and China.³⁵²

### The Development of the Slavic Protestant Movement

The Protestant movement is relatively young in the Slavic world, although the first Protestant church in a Slavic territory was established by Mikolaj Radziwill (1515-1565), the administrative ruler of the Lithuanian Duchy (modern day Lithuania, Belarus, and Poland). Radziwill was a promoter of a Calvinistic faith during his reign, but had his work quickly undone after his death.

The next great Protestant influence among the Eastern Slavs

---

[350] Ware, *The Orthodox Church*. 8. Emphasis in the original.

[351] On December 15, 2018 the local Orthodox Church on the territory of Ukraine was announced which received the name of 'The Orthodox Church of Ukraine'. A Wikipedia article can be found on the following
link: https://en.wikipedia.org/wiki/Orthodox_Church_of_Ukraine . On January 6, 2019 the Orthodox Church of Ukraine was officially given the Patriarchal and Synodal Tomos of Autocephaly (the text can be read on the following link: https://orthodoxyindialogue.com/2019/01/16/tomos-of-autocephaly-the-full-text/. The Russian Orthodox Church (with the seat in Moscow) did not recognize this granting of the Tomos, and broke canonical fellowship with the Constantinopol Church. The Autocephaly of the OCU is partially recognized by other Orthodox Churches.

[352] Ibid., 6.

did not occur until the nineteenth century with the establishment of the first Baptist church in St. Petersburg, Russia, under the direction of Johann Oncken and the development of a Bible publishing house under John Paterson. Both Paterson and Oncken were Calvinists.[353] Oncken, a German Baptist, was tireless in his European missionary activity and was instrumental in establishing churches not only in Germany but in Prussia, Denmark, Austria, Poland, Hungary, Russia, and Turkey.[354]

Additionally, he is credited with founding churches in Finland, Holland, Switzerland, Bulgaria and Africa.[355] H. Leon McBeth referred to Oncken as the "Father of Continental Baptists."[356] Robert G. Torbet acknowledges that it was the missionary zeal of the German Baptist movement under Oncken's influence that was responsible for the Baptist growth on the European continent.[357] Furthermore, McBeth calls Oncken a one-man mission society and says "[s]eldom has one person contributed so much to the development of a denomination…."[358] As a church-planter, he was a strong, Reformed Calvinist.[359] His work in St. Petersburg was

---

[353] David Whitworth, "John Paterson and Ebenezer Henderson," March 2012, https://evangelical-times.org/23016/john-paterson-and-ebenezer-henderson. http://ccggrockford.org/wp-content/uploads/2015/06/Saxon-David-Johan-Gerhard-Oncken-Full-Manuscript.pdf. Paterson trained under Robert and James Haldane and was responsible for founding Bible societies in Finland (1811), Russia (1812), and Sweden (1814).

[354] Thomas Armitage, *The History of the Baptists*, 2 vols. (Watertown, WI: Marantha Baptist Press, 1980), 829.

[355] Saxon, "'Every Baptist a Missionary:' Johann G. Oncken and Disciple-Making in Europe." http://ccggrockford.org/wp-content/uploads/2015/06/Saxon-David-Johan-Gerhard-Oncken-Full-Manuscript.pdf., 12–13. Saxon mentions that he obtained the details regarding Oncken's life from a book written by John Hunt Cooke, *Johann Gerhard Oncken: His Life and Work* (London: S. W. Partridge & Co., 1908).

[356] H. Leon McBeth, *The Baptist Heritage: Four Centuries of Baptist Witness* (Nashville: Broadman, 1987), 470.

[357] Torbet, *A History of the Baptists*, 196.

[358] McBeth, *The Baptist Heritage*, 470.

particularly fruitful with the establishment of a church with four hundred members. This growing church soon experienced great persecution from the Russian Orthodox Church.[360]

Persecution of Eastern Slavic Baptists by the Russian Orthodox Church continued into the 20th century but a new persecutor emerged in the form of the newly formed Soviet state. Under Soviet rule, all who called themselves Christians were considered second class citizens and targeted for persecution by the government.[361] Both the Orthodox churches and the Baptist churches were concerned with survival. This caused two former "enemies" to cooperate with each other to maintain their existence during Soviet rule. Doctrinal purity was replaced with a survival mentality under an atheistic political regime.

Religious publishing houses (both Orthodox and Baptist) among the Eastern Slavs were closed during this era by Soviet authorities. While there were no Eastern Slavic Baptist religious writings to publish, there were also no other Protestant writings in the Slavic languages being published or made available as study resources. As a result, some Baptist ministers have told me that they and their colleagues were using Orthodox study materials in preparation for their messages. What began in the 20th century as a cooperating relationship between the Eastern Orthodox and Baptists in their struggle to survive resulted in an influence of Eastern Orthodox writers on Baptist thinking. But there was a consequence among Slavic Baptists that came from living in an Eastern Orthodox culture and being restricted to Eastern Orthodox theological resources: it made it easier to adopt a man-centered soteriology remarkably similar to that espoused by the early critic of Calvinism, Jacobus Arminius.

It is worth noting here that the Union of Slavic Baptists was

---

[359] Saxon, "Every Baptist a Missionary," 12.

[360] Armitage, *The History of the Baptists*, 829-30.

[361] Tarasenko, "The Historical and Doctrinal Influences of the Russian Orthodox Church," 3.

formed in the nineteenth century. Since the 1800s, in pre-1917 Russia, this was an evangelical movement that united Baptists from Ukraine to St. Petersburg as well as the Caucasus region.[362]

Just prior to the end of World War II in 1944, Slavic Baptists and the denomination known as the "Evangelical Christians" (a predominantly Arminian group led by Ivan Prokhanov), were forced to merge by the Soviet Government to form a union of churches that became known as the All-Union Council of Evangelical Baptists (AUCECB). In 1945, Pentecostal groups (which were relatively small in numbers) were also forced to join the AUECB. Because most Baptist leaders were persecuted and imprisoned, the Evangelical Christians and Pentecostals infused a decidedly Arminian and Pentecostal-leaning theology into a dwindling, Calvinistic, Slavic Baptist ideology.

When was Pentecostalism introduced in the former Soviet Union? Pentecostalism was introduced into the Slavic lands by Alexander Ivanov and Nikolai Smorodln in 1914 when they formed a church in St. Petersburg. Shortly thereafter an association of like-minded churches formed the Society of Evangelical Christians in the Spirit of the Apostles was established (SECSA).[363] This group remained intact until they were forced to merge with the Slavic Baptists in 1944.

The influence of the SECSA's Arminian theology quickly permeated the AUCECB. Arminian theologian Constantine Prokhorov notes that in the 1970s Serzei Petrovich Fadiukin (an AUCECB leader) expressed concern about the teaching of "once saved, always saved" (which, as Wayne Grudem has noted, is one of

---

[362] "Baptist Brotherhood," *EAFECB.com*, accessed January 1, 2020, http://eafecb.com/?page id-514. This information was taken from the website of the All-Union Council of Evangelical Christians-Baptists (ACECB) and translated by Hleb Yermakou, who ministers with Encouragement International, Inc.

[363] Torsten Löfstedt, "Pentecostal and Charismatic Denominations in Russia," *East and West Church Ministry Report*, n.d., accessed January 1, 2021, https://www.eastwestreport.org/38-english/e-19-1/303-pentecostal-and-charismatic-denominations-in-russia.

the hallmarks of Calvinism[364]). He was encouraged by the AUCECB secretary-general at the time (Alexei Bychkov) that the AUCECB did not preach this principle and that the AUCECB was consistent with the teaching of the Word of God.[365] Prokhorov went on to note that this thinking from the Word of God was consistent with the Eastern Orthodox tradition, thus confirming the influence of Eastern Orthodox thinking upon the AUCECB.[366]

After Glasnost in 1987, the AUCECB was restructured and took on a new name—the Union of Evangelical Christian-Baptists (UECB). After the dissolution of the Soviet Union in 1991 the UECB underwent another restructuring that incorporated the new independent bodies that were part of the Commonwealth of Independent States (CIS). This organization was named the Euro-Asian Federation of Unions of Evangelical Christian-Baptists (EAFUECB) in 1992. It is comprised of twelve Unions representing the twelve republics of the former USSR: Ukraine, Russia, Belarus, Moldova, Armenia, Georgia, Azerbaijan, Tajikistan, Uzbekistan, Turkmenistan, Kazakhstan, and Kyrgyzstan. They meet together annually and have a rotating, unelected presidency where one of the Baptist Union presidents (e.g., Ukraine) serves as president of the EAFUECB for one year before passing the presidency to the next in line (e.g., Russia). The EAFUECB also has some loose affiliations with Slavic Baptist churches in Western Europe through some of the twelve National Unions.

## Understanding Arminius and His Influence Among Slavic Baptists

Jacobus Arminius (1560-1609) was a Protestant who had

---

[364] Wayne Grudem, *Systematic Theology*, rev. ed. (Grand Rapids: Zondervan, 2007), 788.

[365] Prokhorov, "Why Russian Baptists Are Neither Arminians nor Calvinists," 206.

[366] Prokhorov., 199, 206.

doubts about the strict Calvinism under which he was raised.[367] Arminius and his followers denied the total depravity of humanity and elevated man's self-determination.[368] This presupposition about the nature of man had an impact on the way justification and grace were understood.

For Arminians, the imputation of Christ's righteousness by grace through faith is actual, not merely forensic. And this imputation begins the transforming work in preparation for being in the presence of God.[369] To arrive at this understanding, Arminians, like Eastern Orthodoxy, have redefined δικαιόω, although in a more subtle way. While Eastern Orthodoxy openly denies the forensic nature of δικαιόω, Arminians accept the forensic nature of δικαιόω but fuse it with sanctification. Arminius did this by saying that justification moved the "declaration and manifestation" of righteousness from the moment of faith to the future general judgment.[370]

The Arminian apologist Roger E. Olson states that "Arminians have always been uncomfortable with a purely forensic (declaratory) righteousness and have attempted to balance that with an inward, imparted righteousness that actually begins to transform a sinner into a righteous person."[371] He also states that Arminius and Luther would agree soteriologically but that Arminians are not as clear regarding the nature of imputed righteousness.[372] This balance comes at the expense of distinctions between δικαιοσύνη and

---

[367] Everett F. Harrison, *Baker's Dictionary of Theology* (Grand Rapids: Baker Academic, 1981), 64.

[368] Harrison, Everett F., 65.

[369] Roger E. Olson, *Arminian Theology* (Downers Grove, IL: IVP, 2006), 201.

[370] W. R. Bagnall, *The Writings of James Arminius*, 3 vols. (Grand Rapids: Baker, 1956), 2:118. The *declaration* is a reference to *justification*, the *manifestation* is a reference to *sanctification*.

[371] Olson, *Arminian Theology*, 201.

[372] Olson, 201–02.

ἁγιασμός and ends up fusing δικαιοσύνη and ἁγιασμός in a way similar to Eastern Orthodox theology.

The atonement, as viewed by Arminians, is merely making salvation possible for man.[373] This is almost identical to Eastern Orthodox thinking. Olson states that the Arminian understanding of the atonement is that Christ's death on the cross not only removes man's penalty for sin, but it also "releases" humanity to reverse its depravity. Both thoughts can be easily harmonized with Eastern Orthodox thinking, and thus are very appealing to Slavic Baptists. The perspective among many Slavic Baptists seems to be that since Arminius was a Protestant, his thinking must be the right kind of Orthodoxy.

## Theological Similarities Between Some Slavic Baptist and The Eastern Orthodox

Earlier it was noted that the Eastern Orthodox concept of *theosis* has changed the Eastern Orthodox understanding of the creation of humanity. They have redefined what it means to be created in the image and likeness of God. Their philosophical understanding of these terms (which ignores the lexical meaning of the words in the biblical passages) resulted in viewing the atonement as the work of Christ that grants man the opportunity to fulfill God's created desire for man (i.e., image). Humanity's desire is to become perfect through significant effort (i.e., likeness). As a result, the imputation of Christ's righteousness is not necessary because man has the ability to become "God-like" through his own efforts after a "push-start" from God. This is the same thinking as the Arminian theology, although would define "image" differently than the Eastern Orthodox.[374]

Thus, both the Eastern Orthodox and Arminian-leaning Slavic Protestants share a propensity to view their salvation as something dependent on their own efforts. Indeed, Phil 2:12 does tell believers

---

[373] Olson., 34.

[374] Harrison, Everett F., *Baker's Dictionary of Theology*, 65. Arminians define image as man's dominion over nature.

to "work out your own salvation." According to Boice, this verse is "problematic for Christians who neglect the context and assume, as a result, that the verse supports the idea of a 'self-help' salvation."[375] When read contextually, this exhortation is not a proof-text for a *theosis* from an Eastern Orthodox perspective or an Arminian explanation of an on-going effort to try really hard to please and find favor with God. While κατεργάζεσθε does mean "to continually work to bring something to fulfillment or completion,"[376] in light of Romans 3:21–24 and Ephesians 2:8–10, κατεργάζεσθε cannot refer to works salvation.[377] Hendriksen connects the understanding of Phil 2:12–13 with John 15:4, where Jesus teaches that His followers cannot bear fruit unless they abide in Him. He states, "So here also. Only then can and do the Philippians work out their own salvation when they remain in living contact with their God. It is exactly because God began an excellent work in them."[378]

Boice adds that Eph 2:8–10 twice mentions works in connection with salvation. In 2:8, man's works before salvation are condemned because the source of the effort is from man. But in 2:10, man's works are the outworking by God in the regenerate which He "prepared in advance for us to do."[379] Philippians 2:12–13, then, refers to a believer's responsibility in sanctification to pursue obedience as a matter of gratitude for justification by grace through faith. As Boice states, the redeemed "work out" what "God has worked in."[380]

---

[375] James Montgomery Boice, *Philippians* (Grand Rapids: Baker, 2000), 142.

[376] William Hendriksen, *Philippians, NTC* (Grand Rapids: Baker Book House, 1975), 120. Hendriksen stresses the use by Paul of the present tense to indicate that "Paul has in mind *continuous, sustained, strenuous effort*: "Continue to work out.""

[377] John MacArthur, *MacNTC* (Nashville: Thomas Nelson Publishers, 2007), 627.

[378] Hendriksen, *Philippians*, 122.

[379] Boice, *Philippians*, 146.

[380] Ibid., 144.

Motivation matters!³⁸¹

This last statement is a vital component to communicate to those in the Slavic culture, whether Eastern Orthodox or Protestant. From their perspective, the purpose of obedience is to secure salvation; it is a journey toward perfection to find favor with God.

But there is a difference between Eastern Orthodox and Arminian Slavic Protestant thinking on this. The Eastern Orthodox assert that *theosis* is an eternal journey—it is a process that begins in this life but does not end until sometime in eternity. No one knows the endpoint of the journey for any one individual. Slavic Protestants, however, understand that *theosis* is complete upon death. For them, being on the journey with a proper confession and proper effort before God in this life finds favor with God and reaps the eternal reward in the next.

Thus, both the Eastern Orthodox and some Slavic Protestants agree on the necessity to find favor with God through one's personal effort in this life, but they disagree on the terminus of the effort. For the Eastern Orthodox, the terminus is nebulous—sometime in the eternal future—evidenced by acquiring enough grace through participation in the sacraments and venerating the icons.³⁸² For Slavic Protestants, the terminus for finding favor is definite—in this life! Their gospel, then, can be appealing to the Eastern Orthodox mind because the attainment of *theosis* is guaranteed in a shorter time period. The effort required to secure this salvation is reduced from an indefinite, even eternal striving, to a definite, temporal one limited to this life.

But finding peace with God through personal effort is abhorrent to God because it is a man-centered and man-glorifying

---

³⁸¹ J.B. Lightfoot, *St. Paul's Epistle to the Philippians* (Grand Rapids: Zondervan Publishing House, 1976), 116. Lightfoot states that Phil 2:12 is "a fusion of two ideas, μὴ ὡς ἐν τῇ παρουσίᾳ μου κατεργάζεσθε and μὴ ἐν τῇ ἀπουσίᾳ μου μόνον κατεργάζεσθε, 'do not be energetic because I am present,' and 'do not be energetic only when I am present.' The pleonastic μὴ lays stress on the sentiment or motive of the agent."

³⁸² Ware, *The Orthodox Church*, 276.

effort. The Eastern Orthodox and some Slavic Protestant gospels are now similar to other world religions. From their perspective, entering into the presence of God is a matter of being put back on the path of correctly pursuing God and living the correct lifestyle. The difference with the world is at the starting point of the process. The world begins with self-effort absent any initial assistance; the Eastern Orthodox and some Slavic Protestants need the work of Christ on the cross to initiate the process.

Why are both abhorrent to God? Because they rob Him of His glory. כָּבוֹד (glory) in the Hebrew[383] and δόξα (glory) in the Greek[384] both carry the idea of "bringing honor." God is noticeably clear that He does not share His glory with anyone (Isa 42:8; 48:11). What is the glory of God is a question that deserves an entire paper unto itself but for now it will need to suffice to make only a few comments as it relates to Jesus' work on the cross.

Paul states in Rom 1:16 that the gospel—not man's efforts—is the power of God for man's salvation. He builds on this argument in Rom 4:20 stating Abraham's belief, or faith, in God's promise of a son (Isaac) was glorifying to God and resulted in his justification. In Rom 5:2, Paul says that a person's hope in Christ's work on the cross glorifies God.

In 1 Cor 1:16, Paul also argues that the cross—not man's effort—is the power of God for man's salvation. Paul doubles down in verse eighteen, stating the cross is God's demonstration of power in the life of the believer in contrast to the non-believer who considers the work of the cross foolish. This statement should strike the conscience of every Eastern Orthodox or Arminian leaning Slavic Baptist and should be developed in any preaching of the gospel among the Slavs.

In Eph 1, God's choice, predestination, and foreknowledge of the elect are cause to praise His glory in the gospel, which is expressed

---

[383] Brown, *BDB,* 458.

[384] *TDNT,* "Δοκέω, Δόξα, Δοξάσω, Συνδοξάζω, Ἔνδοξος, Ἐνδοξάζομαι, Παράδοξος" (Grand Rapids: Eerdmans, 1973), 2:237. Kittel notes the close connection in meaning between כָּבוֹד and δόξα.

through His grace (see verse six specifically). In Phil 1:11, praise and glory are given to God for His work of salvation in the believer's life.

Peter also expresses his understanding that salvation is solely the work of God to His glory. In 1 Pet 1:21, Peter explains that God raised Jesus from the dead and returned Him to the glory which He had before the creation of the world. This work of God, he says, is where Christians are to put their faith and hope—in Jesus' work, not their own! He follows this up in 2 Pet 1:3 where he says it is the divine power that gives us "everything pertaining to life and godliness, through the true knowledge of Him who called us by His own glory and excellence." God's glory is on display in the cross—the cross is His work, His effort, His labor—only a monergistic effort!

Synergism in salvation robs God of His glory. This can be illustrated by the sentiment offered by John Meyendorff, an Eastern Orthodox scholar, who defends synergism by saying, "Since the age of the Fathers the Orthodox church has always upheld the doctrine of synergeia, that is, the collaboration between divine grace and the free will of man on his way toward God. We are all saints by grace, but we must become saints by our acts and in our whole being."[385] This is an anathematized gospel! It is this synergistic understanding of salvation that must be upended in gospel preaching among the Slavs—among the Eastern Orthodox and the Roman Catholics for salvation and among some Slavic Protestants primarily for instruction to correct a faulty biblical understanding of justification and its effects upon the redeemed.

---

[385] Tarasenko, "The Historical and Doctrinal Influences of the Russian Orthodox Church on the Soteriology of the Russian Baptists," 75.

# CHAPTER ELEVEN

## CONCLUSIONS

Eastern Orthodox and some Slavic Protestant theologies are closely and surprisingly aligned. They are both synergistic on justification. Eastern Orthodox synergism is ingrained in their teaching and culture and accepted by some Slavic Protestants. This alignment between the Eastern Orthodoxy and some Slavic Protestants is the result of two influences. First, the Eastern Orthodox Church has a long history in Slavic lands (first established in 988 AD with the conversion of Prince Vladimir). This has resulted in an established religious worldview which has permeated Slavic culture. By contrast, Slavic Protestants have a brief history (19th century to the present). This brief history of Slavic Protestants has resulted in the lack of developed and published doctrine to counter the Eastern Orthodox conceptual thinking that is engrained within their Slavic heritage.

The result of this contrast in history and articulation has been the adoption—with slight modification—of Eastern Orthodox religious thinking by some Slavic Protestants. For example, they share (as does all Christendom) the word "justification." But without distinctively Protestant, exegetical resources, some Slavic Protestants have adopted the Eastern Orthodox concept of justification. Instead of a biblically defined concept of justification as "declared righteousness," they have adopted the corrupted definition by Jerome which was endorsed by John of Damascus and expressed by the Eastern Orthodox as "making or being made righteous."

Secondly, this foreign understanding of justification has been reinforced by the merger of the Slavic Baptists with the Arminian Pentecostal "Evangelical Christians." The sanative understanding of justification embraced by the "Evangelical Christians" is remarkably similar to Eastern Orthodox thinking and quickly dominated the dwindling Calvinistic thinking of the Slavic Baptists. Again, without good exegetical resources, the biblical understanding of salvation, grace, faith, sanctification, and imputation has negative effect on the proper understanding of justification.

Along with this misunderstanding of justification comes the misconception of another soteriological term: grace. Rather than obtaining God's favor through faith alone as defined biblically (Eph 2:8–9; Titus 3:5), "grace" is acquired after significant effort. This again is another adoption of Eastern Orthodox thinking that incorporates the non-Reformational definition and misunderstanding of what it means to be created in the "image" and "likeness" of God.

## A CHALLENGE TO MY READING AUDIENCE

Read the Letter to the Galatians with the proper theological definitions presented earlier in this book.

Texts like Gal 2:16—properly exegeted with properly defined biblical terms—plant the challenge for change in our understanding of what it means to be justified. Similarly, the first five chapters of Romans provide the conviction to upend and exchange misconception for the biblical understanding of these key words for embracing the truth of the gospel. As students of God's Word, we should not assume that our understanding of words like "justification," "sanctification," "salvation," "faith," "grace," and "image and likeness" without proper, biblical definition are conveying saving faith.

# APPENDIX ONE

# TABLE OF JUSTIFICATION USAGE IN THE NEW TESTAMENT

The grammar used by Paul under the inspiration of the Holy Spirit strongly reenforces that δικαιόω is a forensic, monergistic, declaration by God conferred through faith on the redeemed of God.[386] How does the grammar support the lexical concept of divine, forensic, monergistic justification in Pauline writings? The answer comes by understanding the difference between the active and passive voice. The active voice is used to show that the subject is doing the action of the verb. When the subject is God in the discussion of justification, Paul uses the active voice five times in the table below to show that God is doing the work of justification. For example, in Romans 8:30, it says "and whom He predestined, these He also called; and whom He called, these He also justified; and whom He justified, these He also glorified." This is a clear statement that justification is monergistically an action of God on a believing sinner.

The passive voice is used to show that the subject is receiving the action of the verb. When the subject is man in the discussion of justification, Paul uses the passive voice to emphasize that the subject (man) is receiving the action of Divine justification. For example, Galatians 2:16 is correctly translated as "nevertheless knowing that a man is not justified [by God] by works of the Law but through faith in Christ Jesus, even we have believed in Christ Jesus, that we may be justified [by God] by faith in Christ, and not by the works of the Law, since by works of the Law shall no flesh be justified [by God]. Paul, under the inspiration of the Holy Spirit, is making it clear that justification is Divine and without the assistance of man. Or, said in a separate way, it is a *Divinely monergistic* work! Man does not assist in his own justification. Some may say that man assists God's justifying work by believing but Paul dismisses this thought in Ephesians 2:8-9 by saying that man's belief is every bit a gift from

---

[386] See the definition of "Justification" in the Introduction.

God like the grace he receives excluding the possibility of an initiatory act by man to receive the gift of grace. Paul reenforces this thought in Titus 3:4-7 by stating that every component of salvation (specifically, regeneration and justification) is the result of Divine action.

| WORD | V. | T. | V. | MOOD | PERSON | # |
|---|---|---|---|---|---|---|
| δικαιωθήσονται | Rom 2:13 | Future | Passive | Indic. | 3 | p. |
| δικαιωθῇς | Rom 3:4 | Aorist | Passive | Subj. | 3 | p. |
| δικαιωθήσεται | Rom 3:20 | Future | Passive | Indic. | 3 | s. |
| δικαιώσει | Rom 3:30 | Future | Active | Indic. | 3 | s. |
| ἐδικαιώθη | Rom 4:2 | Aorist | Passive | Indic. | 3 | s. |
| δεδικαίωται | Rom 6:7 | Perfect | Passive | Indic. | 3 | s. |
| ἐδικαίωσεν | Rom 8:30 (2) | Aorist | Active | Indic. | 3 | s. |
| δεδικαίωμαι | 1 Cor 4:4 | Perfect | Passive | Indic. | 1 | s. |
| δικαιοῦται | Gal 2:16a | Present | Passive | Indic. | 3 | s. |
| δικαιωθῶμεν | Gal 2:16b | Aorist | Passive | Indic. | 1 | s. |
| δικαιωθήσεται | Gal 2:16c | Future | Passive | Subj. | 3 | p. |
| δικαιοῖ | Gal 3:8 | Present | Active | Indic. | 3 | s. |
| δικαιοῦται | Gal 3:11 | Present | Passive | Indic. | 3 | s. |
| δικαιωθῶμεν | Gal 3:24 | Aorist | Passive | Subj. | 1 | p. |
| δικαιοῦσθε | Gal 5:4 | Present | Passive | Indic. | 2 | p. |
| ἐδικαιώθη | 1 Tim 3:16 | Aorist | Passive | Indic. | 3 | s. |
| PTCP | V. | T. | Vo. | | CASE | GNDR | # |
| δικαιούμενοι | Rom 3:24 | Present | Passive | | Nom. | Masc. | p. |
| δικαιοῦντα | Rom 4:5 | Present | Active | | Acc. | Masc. | s. |
| Δικαιωθέντες | Rom 5:1 | Aorist | Passive | | Nom. | Masc. | p. |
| δικαιωθέντες | Rom 5:9 | Aorist | Passive | | Nom. | Masc. | p. |

| | | | | | | | |
|---|---|---|---|---|---|---|---|
| δικαιῶν | Rom 8:33 | Present | Active | | Nom. | Masc. | s. |
| δικαιωθέντες | Titus 3:7 | Aorist | Passive | | Nom. | Masc. | plural |
| **INF** | **V.** | **T.** | **Vo.** | | | | |
| δικαιοῦσθαι | Rom 3:28 | Present | Passive | | | | |
| δικαιωθῆναι | Gal 2:17 | Aorist | Passive | | | | |

## ABBREVIATIONS

**V. = verse**
**T. = tense**
**Vo. = voice**
**Indic. = indicative**
**Subj. = subjunctive**
**p. = plural**
**s. = singular**
**Nom. = nominative**
**Acc. = accusative**
**PTCP = participle**
**GNDR = gender**
**Masc. = masculine**
**INF = infinitive**

# APPENDIX TWO

## THE EFFECT OF RE-DEFINING JUSITIFICATION ON THE CONCEPT OF ELECTION

This book has attempted to demonstrate that once justification is incorrectly defined, the incorrect definition will have a "snowball" effect on redefining and incorrectly understanding other doctrines related to a biblical understanding of salvation, faith, grace, sanctification, and man being created in the image of God. However, this list of the effects of misunderstanding justification is not complete. Incorrectly defining justification has also resulted in an incorrect understanding of the biblical term election. The monergistic work of justification is sometimes challenged by a works oriented Divine election that is supposedly supported by Divine foreknowledge. This viewpoint takes the monergistic sovereign work of God and reduces this biblical teaching to a synergistic Divine-human work rewarded by God looking ahead in time in order to choose those worthy to be selected. Is this synergistic idea a biblical understanding of Divine election?

### Defining Election

The words translated as chosen and elect (ἐκλέγω, ἐκλογή, ἐκλεκτός) are used twenty-one times in the New testament to describe those who are "saved" or as was defined earlier in this book, "rescued" from God's coming wrath. The basic meaning of the word "chosen," or "elect" is "to pick out,"[387] "to select."[388] The word carries the implication of choosing with "kindness or favor or love."[389] The inherent implication of the word indicates the Divine motive behind "election"—it is Divine love not human merit.

Critical in understanding election is identifying who is doing

---

[387] *EDNTW*, "Choice, Choose, Chosen", 1:189. See also, "Elect", 2:21.

[388] *TDNT*, "ἐκλογή", IV:176, 181.

[389] *EDNTW*, "Choice, Choose, Chosen" 1:189.

the selection or choosing, and who is being chosen or selected. In eighteen of the twenty references it is clear that God is making the selection or choice with the objects being redeemed men (Matthew 24:14, 22, 24, 31; Mark 13:20, 22, 27; Luke 18:7; John 13:18; Romans 11:7; 1 Corinthians 1:27, 28; Colossians 3:12; 2 Timothy 2:10; Titus 1:1; 1 Peter 1:1 and Revelation 17:14.) Only in 2 John 1:1 and 13 is the selector unspecified but implied to be God. What is very evident in these verses is that man is not choosing God! God is choosing and selecting those who will be redeemed. In contrast, man is not—in these passages—identified as choosing or selecting God for redemption.

## Does God Have A Bias In His Selection Of Those He Will Elect To Redemption

The answer to this question has been a matter of debate among the Reformers since the sixteenth century. Does God look ahead in time and make His selection for redemption based upon the actions or beliefs of man, or does God make His selection independent of what He sees men doing and believing? If God is making His selection based upon the actions and beliefs of man, then His selection of a man for redemption is based upon the man's work! This thinking contradicts the clear teaching of Ephesians 2:8,9 and Titus 3:4, 5 which definitively teach that man's work of faith cannot result in justification by God. If then, God is making an independent choice that is not merit based, is there a clear statement in Scripture that verifies this independent and sovereign non-meritorious selection?

Paul gives us the answer to this question in Ephesians 1:4-11 with specific highlights of verses 4, 5 and 11. In his opening remarks to the church in Ephesus, Paul, after his greeting to the Ephesians in 1:1-3, launches into an extended praise of God for His redemptive work (1:4-14). He is not praising the Ephesians for their choice or selection of God for their salvation. Instead, Paul focuses on God's work in the Ephesian believers, and in general, in those who will believe. In verses 1:4-6, Paul praises the Father for His selection of the ones He chose to redeem, in verses 1:7-12, Paul praises God for the work of Christ in redeeming those who were selected to receive redemption, and in verses 1:13-14, Paul praises the work of the Holy Spirit in sealing those selected for redemption as a pledge for their rescue from the coming wrath of God upon the unredeemed.

In Ephesians 1:4-11, Paul uses three words (ἐκλέγω, προορίζω, κληρόω) to express the sovereign, independent selection of sinners by God for redemption. Each use of these words strongly affirms a selection of sinners for redemption that is the independent and sovereign choice of God based upon His purpose and not man's desire or interest. Let's examine these words one at a time to see what they reveal about the sovereign selection by God of sinners for redemption.

Ephesians 1:4 reads: " just as He chose (ἐξελέξατο) us in Him before the foundation of the world, that we should be holy and blameless before Him. In love." (NASB) The first observation to be made in verse four is the word "chosen" (ἐξελέξατο). The fact that the word is in the Greek middle voice tells us much about the one doing the selection. The middle voice describes the subject as one who "participates in the results of the action."[390] God is the subject, and the results are His selection of the redeemed. Paul is very clearly asserting that God (the subject) is personally making the selection of who will be redeemed. He did not consult others before making the selection. It was His independent and sovereign choice.[391] and His selection of men for redemption was not made based upon their observed future merit. As John Eadie has said, "The whole procedure lies in the domain of pure sovereignty, ...."[392] It is an unconditional selection by God.

The second observation to be made is that God made His selection of men for redemption before the foundation of the world.

---

[390] H. E. Dana and Julius R. Mantey, *A Manual Grammar of the Greek New Testament* (Toronto: Macmillan Company, 1957), 157.

[391] John MacArthur, *Ephesians*, The MacArthur New Testament Commentary (Chicago: Moody Press, 1986), 11.

[392] John Eadie, *Commentary on the Epistle to the Ephesians* (Minneapolis, MN: James & Klock Publishing, 1977), 23.

Prior to the universe being created, God's eternal selection of those who would be redeemed was made. As MacArthur has wisely noted, God designed His church before the world began.[393] The necessity of Divine selection prior to creation is captured by Charles Spurgeon as quoted by Henry Ironside. Spurgeon said, "God certainly must have chosen me before I came into this world or He never would have done so afterwards."[394]

A third observation that comes from this verse is the motive for God's selection of those He redeemed to make up His church. It is based upon His love for His creation. In order to appreciate the Divine love of man in election, those who recognize His selection of them must understand how unlovely as sinners they were before their Holy God. Paul, in Romans 5:10, calls non-justified men the enemies of God. The word enemy (ἐχθρός) carries the understanding of "hatred" and "hostility."[395] Murray notes that man's hostility is a passive hostility in contrast to an active hostility.[396] As has been stated earlier in this book, the passive voice is used to describe that the subject as being acted upon. In Romans 5:10, the word "enemies" identifies the subject of the sentence. The verb "reconciled" (κατηλλάγημεν) is in the passive voice indicating the act of reconciling is being performed upon the subject ("enemy). Since God, the outside force, is actively reconciling the enemies to Himself, the enemies (mankind) are passive in the transaction. This indicates that man as the enemy of God is passively receiving the gift of reconciliation from a God who is actively opposing them. This implies that man is not actively opposing God to be His enemy, but that God is opposed to man who is His enemy because of sin. This passive understanding of God's enmity with man in Romans 5

---

[393] MacArthur, *Ephesians*, 13.

[394] H. A. Ironside, *In The Heavenlies* (Neptune, NJ: Loizeaux Brothers, 1975), 25.

[395] *EDNTW*, "Enemy", 2:30.

[396] John Murray, *The Epistle to the Romans*, New International Commentary on the New Testament (Grand Rapids: Eerdmans, 1977), 172.

describes God's hostility and alienation toward those who are not justified by faith in Christ's work.[397] Paul, then, is telling us in Romans 5:10 that the sinner's reconciliation with God is all the more amazing in light of the sinner's alienation from God. In the words of Hendriksen, God's reconciling love is "…unprecedented and unparalleled. No merit from our side could have moved Christ to die for us, for he died for us "while we were still sinners. ""[398] Romans 5 precede this thought:8 which says: "But God demonstrates His own love toward us, in that while we were yet sinners, Christ died for us." (NASB)

A second word used by Paul in Ephesians 1:4-11 describing God's sovereign selection of man for justification is the word προορίζω found in verses 5 and 11. The English versions of Ephesians consistently translate this Greek word as "predestine". The word is a combination of a preposition (προ) and a verb (ορίζω) meaning to mark out or determine beforehand.[399]

What was God's criteria for selecting certain from mankind for justification? The answer is not philosophically derived but contextually determined at the end of verse 4. The phrase "In love" at the end of verse 4 in English translations is the beginning of the sentence found in verse 5 and describes the motivation of God in His selective process. Hendriksen describes the wonder of this Divine motivation as "… his boundless *love*, motivated by nothing outside himself, … [to] set them apart to be his own sons."[400] MacArthur goes on to remind us that "Biblical agape love is not an emotion but a disposition of the heart to seek the welfare and meet the needs of others."[401] God, then, desires to seek the welfare of His rebellious

---

[397] Murray, 172.

[398] William Hendriksen, *Exposition of Paul's Epistle to the Romans* (Grand Rapids: Baker, 1981), 173.

[399] EDNTW, "Determine", 1:305.

[400] William Hendriksen and Simon Kistemaker, *New Testament Commentary* (Grand Rapids, Mich.: Baker Book House, 2007), 79.

[401] MacArthur, *Ephesians*, 14.

creation, but because, as those who are spiritually dead, they are unresponsive to His call and must be made spiritually alive (Ephesians 2:5). But who will be made alive to respond to His call? Those whom He sovereignly selected before the foundation of the world.

Paul reinforces these thoughts at the end of Ephesians 1:5 by stating that God's sovereign selection of those who will be justified is "according to the kind intention of His will,." Again, Hendriksen makes an inciteful comment on Divine sovereign selection when he says, "Hence, what he did was a result not of sheer determination but of supreme delight."[402] This understanding of predestination shows the importance of mining the context to understand doctrinal truths rather than making conclusions based upon philosophical thinking. It is also consistent with the thinking later in Ephesians 2:8, 9 that states predestination is not based upon the good thoughts or actions of man which God looked ahead in time to see before He made His selections. If this were true, then predestining those who would be justified would be based upon those whose actions and thoughts merit God's selection—in short, a works-based rather than a faith-based salvation.

Finally, there is a third word that Paul uses in Ephesians 1:4-11 to emphasize the independent, Divine, sovereign selection of sinners for justification—the word κληρόω. This is the most interesting word of the three that Paul uses to describe Divine selection and strongly emphasizes the Divine, sovereign, independent selection of a sinner for justification. The word's primary meaning is "to cast lots or to choose by lot."[403] The word is only used this one time in the New Testament, but it caps a rich concept in Paul's inspired understanding of divine selection found in Ephesians 1. What is being emphasized by God through Paul with this intriguing word?

In the absence of hearing God's prophetic voice, the will of God was many times determined by the Jews through the casting of lots. The lot was used to determine the Divine selection of:

- Sacrificial animals (Leviticus 16:8-10)

---

[402] Hendriksen and Kistemaker, 79.
[403] EDNTW, *"Heritage,"* 2:217. TDNT affirms this understanding of the word (see 3:764).

- Land portions for the tribes of Israel (Numbers 26:55-56; 33:54; 34:13; 36:2; Joshua 14:2; 16:1; 17:1, 2; Ezekiel 45:1; 47:22; 48:29)
- Identifying sinners (Joshua 7:14)
- Identifying the first king of Israel (1 Samuel 10:20)
- Choosing the high priest for service (Luke 1:9)
- Identifying Matthias as Judas' replacement as an Apostle (Acts 1:26)

The common factor of the lot in each situation is sovereign Divine selection with no pre-conditions in His conclusive determination. In these passages there is no explanation of why God is making His decision, rather, the passages simply state that He is making a sovereign choice. The conclusiveness of this sovereign choice is emphasized in Proverbs 16:33 ("The lot is cast into the lap, But its every decision is from the LORD" (NASB, ESV, NIV) and in Proverbs 18:18 ("The lot puts an end to contentions, And decides between the mighty". (NASB)

But Paul under divine inspiration makes an even stronger case for unconditional Divine selection of those who are justified by using κληρόω ("receiving by lot" or as it has been translated "obtaining an inheritance") in the passive voice. Once again by way of reminder, the passive voice indicates that the subject is being acted upon. As an aorist passive first person plural form of the verb, κληρόω is communicating that the subjects (i.e., those who will be justified) are being acted upon by an outside force or being. The focus is upon the selector not the selected. Furthermore, the word προορίζω, also used in this verse for the second time in this section, is found in the passive voice (an aorist passive participle) again communicating that an outside force or being is acting independently on the subject (i.e., the justified). If the subject is being acted upon, the subject is not the cause of the action—that is, the subject (i.e., the justified) is not being rewarded for an action he has down, instead the subject is the recipient of an action that is conferred upon him by an unbiased decision. Said in a separate way, the subject has no part in the action resulting in a benefit to himself. The context in verse 11 confirms this thinking. The justified are chosen by lot meaning they are predestined according to

God's purpose (not human merit) who works after the counsel of His (God's) will. The emphasis is not on the randomness of God's selection, but on the sovereignty of God's selection. Notice it is God's will—not human merit—that determines who is predestined.

Election like justification is a sovereign, monergistic Divine act. The Divine selection of those who will be justified by faith alone is not influenced by the perceived actions of man in the future if given the opportunity to believe but, according to Paul in Ephesians 1:4-11—who is writing under Divine inspiration—by the independent selection of a sovereign God. It is really easy to understand—God selects many from the "pool" of non-justified to be justified! The motive of His selection is His love (verse 4) and His will (verse 5) according to His good pleasure (verse 5). God is not required to justify any—but He does! And He does so as a gift—and a gift (Ephesians 2:8) cannot be earned otherwise they cease to be gifts!

One final thought. The meaning of election as the independent selection of a sovereign God is supported lexically, grammatically and contextually in God's inspired word. The philosophical idea of a merit's-based election of those who will be justified removes God's Divine, sovereign choice of those who will eternally enter His kingdom. This diminishment of His sovereign control robs God of His glory and God has clearly stated in Isaiah 42:8 and 48:11 that He will not share His glory with anyone. Thus, to reject election as a sovereign, Divine act based upon God's sovereign will motivated by His love and His good intention for those He created is to rob God of His glory in the gospel!

# APPENDIX THREE

## THE EFFECT OF RE-DEFINING JUSTIFICATION ON THE CONCEPT OF ETERNAL SECUTRITY

Not only does the redefinition of justification have an adverse effect upon the biblical understanding of election, but it has an adverse effect on understanding the biblical teaching of the perseverance of the saints also known as eternal security. The theologian Louis Berkhof defines perseverance as "… that continuous operation of the Holy Spirit in the believer by which the work of divine grace that is begun in the heart, is continued and brought to completion."[404] Grudem more succinctly summarizes perseverance by saying that the truly born-again will persevere.[405] Notice in these definitions that the persevering work originates and is sustained by God in man. Does scripture uphold this understanding?

### Who Does The Persevering Work?

R.E.O. White summarized Augustine's thinking by saying that Augustine "traced every thought and motion Godward to the operation of divine grace within those elected to salvation. Nothing was ascribed to human initiative, or even human response."[406] He also noted that Calvin taught that believers are "kept in the faith by the almighty power of God."[407] The biblical stress—initially highlighted by Augustine and re-emphasized by the Reformers—is that perseverance is not initially or primarily a disposition or action of the believer but rather the necessary and continuing work of God.

---

[404] Berkhof, *Systematic Theology*, 546.

[405] Grudem, *An Introduction to Biblical Doctrine*, 788. The full quotation reads: "The perseverance of the saints means that all those who are truly born again will be kept by God's power and will persevere as Christians until the end of their lives, and that only those who persevere until the end have been truly born again."

[406] Walter A. Elwell and Peter Toon, eds., *The Concise Evangelical Dictionary of Theology* (Grand Rapids, Mich: Baker Book House, 1991), 381.

[407] Elwell and Toon, 382.

## Where Does The Bible Support This Concept Of Sovereign Perseverance?

The focus of our answer to this question will be on six strong statements given on perseverance in the New Testament. They are:

- John 10:27-29 where Jesus strongly teaches the protective care of God for His elect.
- 2 Thessalonians 3:3 where Paul teaches that God protects the believer from the evil one (Satan).
- Romans 11:29 where Paul teaches that God's calling is irrevocable.
- Philippians 1:6 where Paul teaches that God completes what He starts.
- 1 Peter 1:5 where Peter teaches that God protects what He has promised to rescue ("save").
- 2 Timothy 1:12 where Paul states that God is able to guard him in his faith until the day he is rescued from God's wrath; and

We will look at two of these statements in more detail and make some summary observations on the other four.

### John 10:27-29

**"My sheep hear My voice, and I know them, and they follow Me; and I give eternal life to them, and they shall never perish; and no one shall snatch them out of My hand. "My Father, who has given *them* to Me, is greater than all; and no one is able to snatch *them* out of the Father's hand. (NASB)**

The words of Jesus in John 10:27-29 are a fitting way to begin this brief study of God's persevering work as proclaimed in the New Testament. After stating that His sheep will know and follow His voice (verse 28), Jesus describes His care for them as eternal (verse 29), and that no one shall (verse 28) or is able (verse 29) to snatch them out of His hand.

It is interesting to note that Origen readily agreed that "no one" is able to snatch the followers of Jesus from His hand. Nonetheless he says, "But we are able to fall from His hands if we are negligent."[408] However, Cyril of Alexandria taught to the contrary. He taught, "For it is not possible that those who are in Christ's hand should be snatched away to be punished because of the great might Christ has. For "the hand" in divine Scripture signifies "the power." It cannot be doubted therefore that the hand of Christ is unconquerable and mighty to all things."[409] Who is correct? Does Jesus teach that His sheep are able to escape from His hand or is His hand strong enough not only to keep the sheep from escaping but also to protect them from being snatched away? Three clues in the passage affirm the teaching of Cyril rather than Origen.

The first clue to comprehending John 10:27-29 is to understand the meaning of the word "eternal" (αἰώνιος). In Greek poetry and prose it was used to describe something enduring or lifelong.[410] The word's predominant use in the New Testament has the concept of "endless" and is used in 2 Corinthians 4:18 as a contrast to the word "temporal" (πρόσκαιρος).[411] In John 10:27-29, Jesus gives His sheep an enduring not a limited promise of protection while they wait for their rescue from the wrath to come.

The second clue to comprehending John 10:27-29 is found in the phrase "shall never perish". The Greek uses a double negative (οὐ μὴ) to convey the impossibility of perishing or losing the eternal life being protected by Jesus in the believer. Friberg's Analytical Greek Lexicon notes that the οὐ denies an alleged fact while the μὴ denies

---

[408] Joel C. Elowsky and Thomas C. Oden, eds., *John 1-10*, Ancient Christian Commentary on Scripture 4a (Downers Grove, Ill: InterVarsity Press, 2006), 357.

[409] Elowsky and Oden, 357.

[410] *TDNT*, "αἰών, αἰώνιος," 2:208.

[411] *EDNTW*, "Eternal," 2:47. Although Vine notes that the word can be used to describe undefined but not endless duration, it is primarily used to describe persons or things that are endless in their nature. An example would be Romans 16:26 where God is describes as "eternal" (αἰώνιος) to describe God as unlimited by time.

the idea.⁴¹² Friberg's lexicon makes an even stronger, grammatical statement when it says that when οὐ μὴ are used in combination, they express a strong negative that should be translated as "never, in no way, under no circumstances, [or] certainly not."⁴¹³ Thus, the Holy Spirit through the Apostle John is conveying the understanding that the idea of a believer losing Jesus' protective promise of being rescued from Divine wrath is factually untrue.

The final clue to comprehending John 10:27-29 is found in the phrases "shall snatch" (ἁρπάσει in verse 28) and "able to snatch " (δύναται ἁρπάζειν in verse 29) to describe Jesus' protective power of the elect. "Snatch" in verse 28 is in the future tense while "snatch" in verse 29 is in the present tense. John is telling his readers that Jesus' persevering protection of His sheep is so secure that no one in the present is able to or in the future will be able to snatch a follower of Jesus from His hands. This thought is intensified in verse 29 because "snatch" is an infinitive and draws its power from the word "able" (δύναται in the Greek). The Greek infinitive can do the work of either a noun or a verb.⁴¹⁴ Its most common usage in the New Testament is verbal and expresses the purpose of the controlling verb. The controlling verb is "able" (δύναται). What purpose is the controlling verb trying to communicate? That no one is "able" (δύναται) to "snatch" (ἁρπάζειν) the sheep from the hand of the Father—He is too powerful to be overcome by any outside force.

Jesus strongly teaches the protective care of God over the elect in John 10:27-29. Once chosen, God's care is eternal (enduring and endless), it is impossible that as those who have been rescued from God's future wrath to experience it, and no one—not even the elect—is powerful enough to open the protective hand of God.

---

⁴¹² Timothy Friberg, Barbara Friberg, and Neva F. Miller, *Analytical Lexicon of the Greek New Testament*, Baker's Greek New Testament Library 4 (Grand Rapids, Mich: Baker Books, 2000), 262.

⁴¹³ Ibid., 262.

⁴¹⁴ Dana and Mantey, *A Manual Grammar of the Greek New Testament*, 214.

## 2 Thessalonians 3:3
## But the Lord is faithful, and He will strengthen
## and protect you from the evil *one*. (NASB)

Paul wrote Second Thessalonians to encourage the Thessalonian church in the midst of persecution. The persecution they experienced caused them to ponder the possibility that they had missed the coming of the Lord to rescue them from His wrath. Comfort and encouragement to believers are the motives of Paul behind this epistle. Paul wrote the third chapter of this book to encourage the Thessalonian believers to wait patiently for Christ's return in the midst of their trial. Not only does Paul request their prayers for Divine rescue from his trial but he encourages the Thessalonians that God will provide protection for the Thessalonians not only at the present time in their trial but protection from the eternal damning work of the evil one. He uses three words to describe the Divine protection promised by God—the words faithful, strengthen and protect. What do these words tell us about the persevering work of God in man?

The first word we will examine is the word "strengthen" (στηρίξει). The word means "to make fast; immovable."[415] Although the persecution of the Thessalonian believers is causing turmoil in the church, Paul assures them that the cause of the turmoil cannot overcome the immovable, protective power of God. Their faith in God's rescue from His future wrath is secure in His hands.

The second word Paul uses to reenforce this thought is "protect," "guard," or "keep" (φυλάξει). The idea inherent in the word is the activity of a watchman whose job it is to protect persons or property.[416] Paul is telling the Thessalonians that God will protect like a watchman His elect from all outside threats.

The third word to describe the protective care of God for His elect is the word "faithful" (Πιστὸς). To be described as faithful using

---

[415] TDNT, "στηρίζω," 7:253.

[416] TDNT, "φυλάσσω," 9:236.

this Greek word means to describe someone who is to be trusted and who is reliable.[417] In 2 Thessalonians 3:3 the word "faithful" is used to describe God. Paul, therefore, is comforting the Thessalonians by reminding them of God's immovable reliability to protect the relationship He has established with His people.

This verse is a strong verse for describing the persevering work of God in a believer because the immovable reliability of God to protect the relationship He has established with His people cannot, according to the verse, be overcome by the evil one. No one is more reliable or more powerful than God and on the basis of this truth Paul is offering comfort and encouragement to the Thessalonian church in the midst of the challenge to their faith under their present circumstances. 2 Thessalonians 3:3 is a promise that the Lord will strengthen and protect His church from the evil one.[418]

## Romans 11:29
### for the gifts and the calling of God are irrevocable. (NASB)

Although the context of Romans 11:29 is speaking of God's future plans and promise to restore Israel to usefulness for His kingdom purposes after being set aside during the gospel age, this specific statement regarding Israel has general implications for all the chosen of God. The word irrevocable (ἀμεταμέλητα) used to describe God's faithfulness to Israel has the meaning of "without change of purpose."[419] The word comes from the Greek word for repentance (μεταμέλομαι) which describes having a different feeling about something."[420] The alpha prefix before the word negates the meaning to describe in Romans 11:29 that God has not changed His feeling or purposes for Israel. This would be very encouraging news to any

---

[417] EDNTW, "Faithful," 2:72.

[418] TDNT, "φυλάσσω," 9:241.

[419] EDNTW, "Repent," 2:280.

[420] TDNT, "μεταμέλομαι," 4:626.

Israelite in light of Jeremiah 31:35-40 because Paul is telling his readers of God's faithfulness and reliability to His promise toward them.[421] This should also be an encouraging truth to every believer in light of Romans 8:31-39.

## Philippians 1:6
***For I am* confident of this very thing, that He who began a good work in you will perfect it until the day of Christ Jesus. (NASB)**

Who is the "He," what is the good work and when will it be completed? The Greek grammar and context are truly clear in this verse. God is the "He" (see verse one), the good work is salvation (see verse 5) which will be completed at the coming of Jesus. Dr. Robert Gromaki summarizes this very well when he says, "God did the work. The verbal construction ("he which hath begun") points to Gods personal involvement in their lives. ... the "good work" refers to the applied benefits of salvation secured by the gracious provision of Christ's substitutionary atonement."[422] He also notes that the sphere of operation was in the life of every believer that is evidenced by the preposition "in" (en).[423] What God begins He completes or finishes!

## 1 Peter 1:5
**who are protected by the power of God through faith for a salvation ready to be revealed in the last time. (NASB)**

The entire section of 1 Peter 1:3-9 is a clear and important statement regarding our salvation through faith in the work of Jesus Christ. Kistemaker says "In this particular verse every word is significant ...."[424] The word protected or guarded (φρουρέω) in verse

---

[421] TDNT, 4:629.

[422] Dr. Robert Gromaki, *Stand Fast in Liberty* (The Woodlands, TX: Kress Christian Publishers, 2002), 40.

[423] Gromaki, 40.

[424] Hendriksen and Kistemaker, *New Testament Commentary,* 44.

5 is a military term meaning "to keep under guard."[425] Kistemaker notes that this military term can mean either "to protect someone from danger" or "to prevent someone from escaping."[426] This dual meaning is another way of stating the truth by Jesus in John 10:29. Our faith for the salvation from God's wrath that is coming is protected by the power of God. Rather than hoping we will have the strength to believe through the last times, Peter is telling us that God is powerful enough to protect the faith He has placed within each believer. MacArthur calls this protective Divine power "the sovereign omnipotence that continuously protects His elect."[427] Vine adds that this word is "used of the security of the Christian until the end, ..."[428]

This same idea although using a different Greek word for *"guard"* is expressed in 2 Timothy 1:12 (see the discussion for "guard" back at 2 Thessalonians 3:3). Philip H. Towner strengthens the teaching of the persevering work of God in man when commenting on this verse by observing "that God is the one who is to guard the deposit,"[429] the deposit being the confidence in the gospel that entrusts salvation in God's promise of deliverance from His wrath for sin.

## Conclusion

As the Author of salvation (Hebrews 2:10), we are told in John 10:27-29; 2 Thessalonians 3:3; Romans 11:29; Philippians 1:6; 1 Peter 1:5 and 2 Timothy 1:12 that God is the protector of this salvation in His chosen ones. He will persevere His salvific work in them. The confidence (faith) that is necessary for salvation is a confidence in God's future deliverance from the coming wrath He will unleash on His creation (Revelation 6-19). If we cannot save ourselves because of the weakness of our flesh (Romans 6:19) we certainly are too weak

---

[425] EDNTW, *"Guard"* 2:183.

[426] Hendriksen and Kistemaker, *New Testament Commentary,* 44.

[427] John MacArthur, *1 Peter*, The MacArthur New Testament Commentary (Chicago: Moody Publishers, 2004), 36.

[428] EDNTW, *"Guard,"* 2:183.

[429] Towner, *The Letters to Timothy and Titus,* 476.

to keep ourselves in the protective care of God. He has exerted significant effort to secure salvation through Jesus' work on the cross and even more effort to regenerate man for salvation through the Holy Spirit. He is not going to entrust these precious works by His Son and His Spirit to frail man. He will protect and maintain the work He began until the final deliverance into His presence. This is the message we have seen in these verses. This is the protective power of God that keeps anyone from stealing a believer from His care and keeps any believer from escaping His protective grasp.

*Soli Deo Gloria*

# APPENDIX FOUR

## Table of Comparisons

|  | Bible | Eastern Orthodoxy | Roman Catholicism | Arminian Theology |
|---|---|---|---|---|
| Justification | Reckoned by Forensic Declaration | Forensic fiction Fused with Sanctification | Fused with Sanctification | Forensic declaration Fused with Sanctification |
| Justification | Divine monergism | Divine initiation Human completion | Divine initiation Human completion | Divine initiation Human completion |
| Imputation | Reckoned | Infused Process | Infused Process | Infused Process |
| Salvation Past | Divine monergism Penalty of sin fully paid | Divine Initiation | Divine Initiation | Divine Initiation |
| Salvation Present | Synergism Power of sin is broken in the redeemed | synergism | synergism | synergism |
| Salvation Future | Divine monergism (glorification) Presence of sin finally removed | Continuing synergistic process | Continuing synergistic process | Divine Monergistic reward |
| Sanctification Past | Positional Monergism Penalty of sin is fully paid | Infused at justification | Infused at justification | Infused at justification |
| Sanctification Present | Progressive synergism Power of sin is broken in the redeemed | Human emphasized synergism (theosis) | Human emphasized synergism | Human emphasized synergism |
| Sanctification Future | Perfected monergism Presence of sin is finally removed | Eternal synergistic effort (theosis) | Eternal synergistic effort | Divine monergistic reward |

| | | | | |
|---|---|---|---|---|
| Grace | Monergistic favor | Synergistic energies of God | Conditional Divine Favor | Synergistic favor |
| Faith | Monergistic confidence | Synergistic confidence | Synergistic insecurity | Synergistic insecurity |
| Image of God | Structural Character | Propensity to seek perfection | Structural Character | Structural Character |
| Likeness of God | Structural Character | Perfection accomplished with great effort | Structural Character | Structural Character |
| Election | Divine Monergistic selection | Divine confirmation of human selection | Divine Confirmation of Human selection | Monergistic foreknowledge |
| Perseverance | Monergistic effort | Synergistic work | Synergistic work | Synergistic effort |

# ABOUT THE AUTHOR

I have been ministering among the Slavic Baptists since 1994. In those early days, I had the privilege of serving as an evangelist in outreach for a project known as the Convocation in the CIS (Commonwealth of Independent States) after the breakup of the former Soviet Union.[430] The convocation laid a foundation with the gospel within the CIS that was followed by a project known as The CoMission, a project similar to a Fundamentals of the Faith program.

After participating in four convocations over two years, I was recruited to teach at a newly founded Bible college in Moscow. The first course I taught was entitled "Church History from the Reformation to the Modern Era." The three weeks of teaching from 9 AM to 3 PM daily to enthusiastic students fueled my desire to return the following year. There was only one problem: the church history course I desired to teach (along with every other Bible course at this Bible college) had already been assigned to other interested pastor-teachers. In fact, there was not an opening to teach at the college for another three years!

I pressed the administrator of the college, and he revealed there was another course they were struggling to fill with an instructor. This course was on Eastern and Russian church history and theology. It had been originally developed by an American pastor who had immersed himself in Russian Orthodox church history and theology to prepare for teaching the course in Moscow. He taught

---

[430] Bruce Wilkinson, *The CoMission* (Chicago: Moody, 2004), 26. The convocation was a four-day conference used by The CoMission to lay a foundation for future work with CIS public school teachers. The countries of the former Soviet Union were concerned about the lack of character and morals among their students and sought American Protestant assistance to overcome this deficiency. To the credit of The CoMission leadership, they told the educational leaders of the CIS that there could be no lasting character and moral change within the individuals being targeted unless there was an initial spiritual transformation accomplished by embracing the gospel by faith. The leaders of the CIS agreed to allow the gospel to be presented and a five-year agreement was signed allowing the Convocation thirteen teams per year composed of forty to seventy American pastors, evangelists, and schoolteachers to conduct convocations throughout the CIS.

once but was unable to return. They were searching for the right candidate who knew both biblical theology and Eastern Orthodoxy. While I knew biblical theology, I had only a scant understanding of Eastern Orthodox thinking. After much discussion, an agreement for me to teach was arranged contingent upon passing an oral interview with the American pastor who had pioneered the course. A telephone interview was arranged, and after two hours of theological grilling I was given permission to teach the course.

Over the next several months I immersed myself in Eastern Orthodoxy. I read the books recommended by my interviewer from both Eastern Orthodox authors and Protestant writers critiquing Eastern Orthodox thinking. I attended Eastern Orthodox church services. I interviewed Eastern Orthodox priests. One of my Eastern Orthodox examiners in the United States was Peter Gillquist, one of seven former Campus Crusade for Christ missionaries who converted to Eastern Orthodoxy in the 1970s.[431] After our three-hour in-person conversation, Gillquist told me my understanding of Eastern Orthodox theology was such that when I was ready to convert, he personally would ordain me as a priest. After a year of study and preparation, this confirmed to me that I was finally ready to teach the course, "Eastern and Russian Church History and Theology."

Once I began teaching, the Bible college in Moscow did not want anyone else to teach the course. In fact, they recommended that I teach the course to sister training programs located in Minsk and Kyiv. My understanding of Eastern Orthodox theology made my teaching of Eastern Orthodoxy as an American Protestant a valuable resource to the Slavic Baptist community.

During the first three years of teaching at the Bible college in Moscow, I would take my students, around fifty per class, to the Danilov Monastery. This monastery is the premier Russian Orthodox training center as well as the residence of the patriarch of the Russian Orthodox Church. We were given tours guided and taught by Eastern Orthodox adherents. These tours served two purposes. The first was

---

[431] Peter E. Gillquist, *Becoming Orthodox* (Ben Lemond, CA: Conciliar Press, 1992), 15.

to instill confidence within my students that the course represented Eastern Orthodoxy fairly. The second was to further refine my own understanding of Eastern Orthodox thinking.

At the end of our first trip to the Danilov Monastery, our Orthodox guide came running after me—outside without a coat in the middle of the Russian winter—to thank me for coming to Moscow and to ask me to return often because she had never had such knowledgeable students on Orthodox thinking. But it was in these interactions with the Bible college students that I observed their difficulty in discerning the difference between Eastern Orthodox and biblical thinking on justification. To this day, this difficulty remains evident among some of the Protestant groups to whom I minister.

Encouragement International, Inc. is a religious non-profit organization I founded in response to this difficulty in 1997, for which I serve as president. It is located in Northridge, California. While I reside in California seven months of the year, I travel at the invitation of Slavic churches in Russia, Belarus, Ukraine, Poland, the Czech Republic, France, Portugal, and Australia as well as churches in Sweden, Moldova, Romania and Lithuania during the other five months of the year.

Harrison (Hal) L Hays IV earned a BA (1977 - Religious studies major, Microbiology minor, Organic Chemistry minor) from Wichita State University, a MDIV from Talbot Theological Seminary (1980) and a DMIN from The Masters Seminary (2021). His dissertation is titled ***The Influence of Eastern Orthodoxy Theology on the Slavic Baptist Understanding of Justification by Faith Alone.***

# BIBLIOGRAPHY

Abbott-Smith, G. *A Manual Greek Lexicon of the New Testament*. Edinburgh: T&T Clark, 1973.

Aland, Barbara, Kurt Aland, Johannes Karavidopoulos, Carlo M. Martini, and Bruce M. Metzger. *The Greek New Testament*. Fourth Edition. Stuttgart: United Bible Societies, 2001.

Allison, Gregg R. *Historical Theology*. Grand Rapids: Zondervan, 2011.

———. *The Baker Compact Dictionary of Theological Terms*. Grand Rapids: Baker, 2016.

Andrews, E. A. *Latin-English Lexicon*. New York: Harper & Brothers, 1877.

Aquilina, Mike. *The Fathers of the Church*. Huntington, IN: Our Sunday Visitor, 1999.

Armitage, Thomas. *The History of the Baptists*. 2 vols. Watertown, WI: Maranatha Baptist Press, 1980.

Ash, Christopher. *Teaching Romans*. 2 vols. London: Proclamation Trust Media, 2009.

Bagnall, W.R. *The Writings of James Arminius*. 3 vols. Grand Rapids: Baker, 1956.

Bainton, Roland H. *Here I Stand: A Life of Martin Luther*. Nashville: Abingdon-Cokesbury Press, 1950.

Baker, Matthew, and Todd Speidell. *T. F. Torrance and Eastern Orthodoxy*. Eugene, OR: Wipf & Stock, 2015.

Bamberger, Bernard J. *Leviticus*. Vol. 3. NY: Union of American Hebrew Congregations, 1979.

"Baptist Brotherhood," 2020. http://eafecb.com/?page id-514.

Barclay, William. *The Acts of the Apostles*. The Daily Study Bible Series. Philadelphia: Westminster Press, 1955.

———. *The Letters to the Galatians and Ephesians*. Philadelphia: Westminster Press, 1958.

Barnett, Paul William. *Romans*. Fearn, Scotland: Christian Focus, 2003.

Barrett, Matthew. *Forty Questions About Salvation*. Grand Rapids: Kregel, 2018.

———. *The Doctrine on Which the Church Stands or Falls*. Wheaton, IL: Crossway, 2019.

Barrick, William. "The Mosaic Covenant." *The Master's Seminary Journal* 10, no. 2 (Fall 1999).

Bartos, Emil. *Deification in Eastern Orthodox Theology*. Eugene, OR: Wipf & Stock, 1999.

Bavinck, Herman. *Reformed Dogmatics*. Grand Rapids: Baker, 2001.

Beale, David. *Historical Theology*. Greenville, SC: Bob Jones University Press, 2013.

Beilby, James K., and Paul Rhodes Eddy. *Justification Five Views*. Downers Grove, IL: InterVarsity Press, 2011.

Berkhof, L. *Systematic Theology*. Grand Rapids: Eerdmans, 1977.

Bishop Alexander, Ed., trans. by Karyn I Michael Grigoriev, and edited by Natalia Semyanko. *The Origins of the World and Mankind: An Attempt to Reconcile the Biblical Account with Scientific Discoveries*. La Canada, CA: Holy Trinity Orthodox Monastery, 2004.

Black, David Alan. *Learn To Read New Testament Greek*. Nashville: B&H Publishing Group, 2009.

Boettner, Loraine. *Studies in Theology*. Phillipsburg, NJ: P&R Publishing Co., 1976.

Boice, James Montgomery. *ACTS*. Grand Rapids: Baker, 1997.

———. *Philippians*. Grand Rapids: Baker Books, 2000.

———. *Romans*. 4 vols. Grand Rapids: Baker, 1992.

Braun, Jon E. *Divine Energy*. Ben Lomond, CA: Conciliar Press, 1991.

Bray, Gerald Lewis. *Biblical Interpretation Past & Present*. Downers Grove, Illinois: InterVarsity Press, 1996.

———. *Commentaries on Romans and 1-2 Corinthians*. Ancient Christian Texts. Downers Grove, IL: InterVarsity Press, 2009.

———. *Romans*. Downers Grove, IL: InterVarsity Press, 1998.

Brown, Francis. *BDB*. Peabody, MA: Hendrickson Publishers, 1979.

Bruce, F. F. *The Book of the Acts*. The New International Commentary on the New Testament. Grand Rapids:

Eerdmans, 1976.

Bruce, F.F. *The Epistle to the Galatians*. Grand Rapids: Eerdmans, 1982.

———. *The New Testament Documents*. 6th Edition. Grand Rapids: Eerdmans, 1981.

Buchanan, James. *The Doctrine of Justification*. Grand Rapids: Baker, 1997.

Busenitz, Nathan. *Long Before Luther*. Chicago: Moody Publishers, 2017.

Bush, George. *Notes on Genesis*. 2 vols. Minneapolis: James & Klock Publishing, 1979.

———. *Notes on Leviticus*. Minneapolis: James & Klock Publishing, 1976.

Calvin, Jean. *Institutes of the Christian Religion*. Peabody, MA: Hendrickson Publishers, 2008.

Calvin, John. *Commentary on the Epistles of Paul the Apostle to the Romans*. Vol. 19. Grand Rapids: Baker, 2005.

———. *Commentary on the Epistles of Paul to the Galatians and the Ephesians*. Vol. 21. Grand Rapids: Baker, 2005.

———. *Sermons on Galatians*. Audubon, NJ: Old Paths Publications, 1995.

Clendenin, Daniel B. *Eastern Orthodox Christianity: A Western Perspective*. Grand Rapids, Mich: Baker Books, 1994.

———. *Eastern Orthodox Theology*. 2nd ed. Grand Rapids: Baker, 2003.

———. *Eastern Orthodox Theology: A Contemporary Reader*. Grand Rapids: Baker, 1995.

Dana, H. E., and Julius R. Mantey. *A Manual Grammar of the Greek New Testament*. Toronto: Macmillan Company, 1957.

Demarest, Bruce. *The Cross and Salvation*. Wheaton, IL: Crossway, 2006.

DeSilva, David A. *The Letter to the Galatians*. New International Commentary on the New Testament. Grand Rapids: Eerdmans, 2018.

Doriani, Daniel M. *James*. Reformed Expository Commentary. Philipsburg, New Jersey: P&R Publishing Co., 2007.

Douglas, J. D. *New Bible Dictionary*. 2nd Edition. Wheaton, IL: Tyndale, 1982.

Douglas, J. D., and Merrill C. Tenney. *The New International Dictionary of the Bible*. Grand Rapids: Zondervan, 1987.

Dunn, James D. G. *Romans*. 2 vols. Word Biblical Commentary. Dallas: Word Books, 1988.

Eadie, John. *Commentary on the Epistle to the Ephesians*. Minneapolis, MN: James & Klock Publishing, 1977.

Edwards, Mark J. *ACCS*. 12 vols. Downers Grove, IL: InterVarsity Press, 1998.

Edwards, Mark J. *Galatians, Ephesians, Philippians*. Vol. New Testament VI. Ancient Commentary on Scripture. Downers Grove, Illinois: InterVarsity Press, 1998.

Elowsky, Joel C. *ACCS*. Vol. IVa. Downers Grove, IL: InterVarsity Press, 2006.

———. *ACCS*. Downers Grove, IL: InterVarsity Press, 2006.

Elowsky, Joel C., and Thomas C. Oden, eds. *John 1-10*. Ancient Christian Commentary on Scripture 4a. Downers Grove, Ill: InterVarsity Press, 2006.

Elwell, Walter A., and Peter Toon, eds. *The Concise Evangelical Dictionary of Theology*. Grand Rapids, Mich: Baker Book House, 1991.

Encyclopaedia Britannica. "Slav," May 2020. https://www.britannica.com/topic/Slav.

Erickson, Millard J. *Christian Theology*. Second. Grand Rapids: Baker, 1998.

Fairbairn, Donald. *Eastern Orthodoxy Through Western Eyes*. Louisville, KY: Westminster John Knox Press, 2002.

Fedorov, Vladimir. "Barriers to Ecumenism: An Orthodox View from Russia." *Religion, State & Society*, no. Vol.26(2), p.129 (June 1998).

Florovsky, F. George. "The Ascetic Ideal and the New Testament Reflections on the Critique of the Theology of the Reformation," n.d. http://www.romanity.org/htm/flo.01.en.the_ascetic_ideal_and_the_new_testament.01.htm.

Frame, John. *Systematic Theology: An Introduction to the Christian Faith*. Phillipsburg, NJ: P&R Publishing Co., 2103.

Friberg, Timothy, Barbara Friberg, and Neva F. Miller. *Analytical Lexicon of the Greek New Testament*. Baker's Greek New Testament Library 4. Grand Rapids, Mich: Baker Books, 2000.

Garagin, Michael. "The Oxford Encyclopedia of Ancient Greece and Rome." In *Alexandria*. Vol. 1. Oxford: Oxford, 2010.

Gibbs, Josiah W. *A Manual Hebrew and English Lexicon*. New Haven: Hezekiah Howe, 1832.

Gifford, E. H. *Romans*. Minneapolis, MN: The James Family, 1977.

Gillquist, Peter E. *Becoming Orthodox*. Ben Lemond, CA: Conciliar Press, 1992.

Gower, Ralph. *The New Manner and Customs of Bible Times*. Chicago: Moody Press, 1987.

Green, Lowell C. "Faith, Righteousness, and Justification: New Light on Their Development Under Luther and Melanchton." *The Sixteenth Century Journal* 4, no. 1 (April 1973): 65–86.

Green, Michael. *The Second Epistle of Peter and the Epistle of Jude*. Tyndale New Testament Commentaries. Grand Rapids: Eerdmans, 1979.

Gromaki, Dr. Robert. *Stand Fast in Liberty*. The Woodlands, TX: Kress Christian Publishers, 2002.

Grudem, Wayne. *Systematic Theology*. Revised. Nottingham, England: IVP, 2007.

Guthrie, Donald. *New Testament Introduction*. Downers Grove, IL: InterVarsity, 1968.

Hall, David W., and Peter A. Lillback. *A Theological Guide To Calvin's Institutes*. Phillipsburg, NJ: P&R Publishing Co., 2008.

Hamilton, Jr., James M. *What Is Biblical Theology?* Wheaton, Illinois: Crossway, 2014.

Harakas, Stanley S. *The Orthodox Church: 455 Questions and Answers*. Minneapolis: Light & Life Publishing, 1988.

Harris, Mark J. "Historical Perspectives on the Evangelistic Theology and Methodology of Russian Baptists," 1999.

http://cvi2.org/pages/harris/harris_russian_baptist_evangelistic_history_1999.pdf.

Harrison, Everett F. *Baker's Dictionary of Theology*. Grand Rapids: Baker, 1981.

Hartman, L. F., B. F. Peebles, and M. Stevenson. "New Catholic Encyclopedia." In *Vulgate*, 14:591–600. NY: Thomson Gale, 2003.

Hendriksen, William. *Exposition of Paul's Epistle to the Romans*. Grand Rapids: Baker, 1981.

———. *Galatians*. NTC. Grand Rapids: Baker, 1975.

———. *Philippians*. Grand Rapids: Baker Book House, 1975.

Hendriksen, William, and Simon Kistemaker. *New Testament Commentary*. Grand Rapids, Mich.: Baker Book House, 2007.

Hiebert, D. Edmond. *The Epistles of James*. Chicago: Moody Press, 1979.

Hill, Robert C., trans. *Fathers of the Church*. Vol. 82. Washington, DC: The Catholic University of American Press, 1990.

Hodge, Charles. *Romans*. Wheaton, IL: Crossway, 1993.

———. *Systematic Theology*. Vol. 3. 3 vols. Grand Rapids: Eerdmans, 1995.

———. *Systematic Theology*. Vol. 2. 3 vols. Grand Rapids: Eerdmans, 1995.

———. *Systematic Theology*. Vol. 1. 3 vols. Grand Rapids: Eerdmans, 1995.

Hopko, Protopresbyter Thomas. "The Orthodox Faith." In *Cyril Lukaris*. Vol. 3, 1981. https://www.oca.org/orthodoxy/the-orthodox-faith/church-history/seventeenth-century/cyril-lukaris.

Hornblower, Simon, and Antony Spawforth. "The Oxford Classical Dictionary." In *Alexandria*. Oxford: Oxford, 1996.

Ironside, H. A. *In The Heavenlies*. Neptune, NJ: Loizeaux Brothers, 1975.

Jewell, Elizabeth J., ed. *The Oxford American Desk Dictionary and Thesaurus*. 2nd ed. New York: Berkley Books, 2001.

John MacArthur and Richard Mayhue. *Biblical Doctrine: A*

*Systematic Summary of Bible Truth*. Wheaton, IL: Crossway, 2017.

Johnstone, Robert. *Lectures on the Book of Philippians*. Minneapolis, MN: Klock & Klock, 1977.

Keating, Daniel A. "Divinization in Cyril: The Appropriation of Divine Life." In *The Theology of St. Cyril of Alexandria: A Critical Appreciation*, edited by Thomas Weinandy and Daniel A. Keating. London: T&T Clark, 2003.

Keating, Daniel A., and Thomas G. Weinandy. *The Theology of St. Cyril of Alexandria, A Critical Appraisal*. London: T&T Clark, 2003.

Kistemaker, Simon J. *Peter and Jude*. Baker Book House Company, 1988.

Kittel, Gerhard. "TDNT." In Δοκέω, Δόξα, Δοξάσω, Συνδοξάζω, Ἔνδοξος, Ἐνδοξάζομαι, Παράδοξος, 2:232–55. Grand Rapids: Eerdmans, 1973.

———. *TDNT*. 10 vols. Grand Rapids: Eerdmans, 1976.

Kubo, Sakae. *A Reader's Greek-English Lexicon of the New Testament and a Beginner's Guide for the Translation of New Testament Greek*. Grand Rapids: Zondervan, 1975.

Lane, Anthony N. S. *Justification by Faith in Catholic-Protestant Dialogue: An Evangelical Assessment*. London: T&T Clark, 2002.

Le Goff, Jacques. *The Birth of Purgatory*. Chicago: University of Chicago Press, 1984.

Leeuwen, Th.Marius van, Keith D. Stanglin, and Marijke Tolsma. *Arminius, Arminianism, and Europe*. Boston: Brill, 2009.

Letham, Robert. *Systematic Theology*. Wheaton: Crossway, 2019.

Lewis, Charlton T. *A Latin Dictionary*. Oxford: Clarendon, 1980.

Lightfoot, J. B. *The Epistle of St. Paul to the Galatians*. Grand Rapids: Zondervan, 1976.

Lightfoot, J.B. *St. Paul's Epistle to the Galatians: With Introductions, Notes, and Dissertations*. Andover, MA: Hendrickson Publishers, 1891.

———. *St. Paul's Epistle to the Philippians*. Grand Rapids: Zondervan Publishing House, 1976.

Löfstedt, Torsten. "Pentecostal and Charismatic Denominations in Russia." *East and West Church Ministry Report* (blog), n.d. https://www.eastwestreport.org/38-english/e-19-1/303-pentecostal-and-charismatic-denominations-in-russia.

Longenecker, Richard N. *Galatians*. Dallas: Word Books, 1990.

Longman III, Tremper. "The Baker Compact Bible Dictionary." In *Impute, Imputation*. Grand Rapids: Baker, 2014.

Lossky, Vladimir. *Orthodox Theology*. Crestwood, NY: St. Vladimir's Seminary Press, 1978.

Lossky, Vladimir. *Orthodox Theology: An Introduction*. Crestwood, NY: St. Vladimir's Seminary Press, 1978.

Louth, Andrew. *Introducing Eastern Orthodox Theology*. Downers Grove, IL: InterVarsity Press, 2013.

Luther, Martin. *Commentary on the Epistles to the Romans*. Grand Rapids: Kregel, 1978.

———. *Galatians*. Wheaton: Crossway, 1998.

———. *Lectures on Galatians*. Luther's Works. St. Louis: Concordia, 1963.

———. *Luther: Lectures on Romans*. The Library of Christian Classics. Philadelphia: Westminster, 1961.

Lykhosherstov, Oleksandr. "The Impact of Orthodox Church Tradition-as-Authority on the Identity and Theology of Evangelical Christians in the Commonwealth of Independent States." *Theological Reflections* 14 (2013): 163–83.

MacArthur, John. *1 Peter*. The MacArthur New Testament Commentary. Chicago: Moody Publishers, 2004.

———. *2 Peter & Jude*. MNTC. Chicago: Moody Press, 2005.

———. *Ephesians*. The MacArthur New Testament Commentary. Chicago: Moody Press, 1986.

———. *Galatians*. MNTC. Chicago: Moody Press, 1987.

———. *James*. MNTC. Chicago: Moody Press, 1998.

———. "Reexamining the Eternal Sonship of Christ," n.d. https://www.gty.org/library/articles/A235/reexamining-the-eternal-sonship-of-christ.

———. *Revelation 12-22*. MNTC. Chicago: Moody Press, 2000.

———. *Romans*. MNTC. Chicago: Moody Press, 1991.

MacArthur, John. *The MacArthur New Testament Commentary*. Nashville, TN: Thomas Nelson Publishers, 2007.

Mandryk, Jason. *Operation World*. 7th ed. Colorado Springs, CO: Biblica Publishing, 2010.

Mantzaridis, Georgios I. *The Deification of Man*. Crestwood, NY: St. Vladimir's Seminary Press, 1984.

Martin, Francis. *ACTS*. Ancient Christian Commentary on Scripture. Downers Grove, IL: InterVarsity, 2006.

Maxwell, David R. "Justification in the Early Church." *Concordia Journal* 44, no. 3 (2018): 25–40.

McBeth, H. Leon. *A Sourcebook For Baptsit Heritage*. Nashville: Broadman & Holman, 1990.

———. *The Baptist Heritage*. Nashville: Broadman, 1987.

McCarthy, James G. *The Gospel According to Rome*. Eugene, OR: Harvest House Publishers, 1995.

McDowell, Josh. *Evidence That Demands a Verdict*. Vol. 1. 2 vols. Nashville: Thomas Nelson Publishers, 1979.

McDowell, Josh. *The New Evidence That Demands A Verdict*. Nashville: Thomas Nelson Publishers, 1999.

McGrath, Alister E. "Forerunners of the Reformation? A Critical Examination of the Evidence for Precursors of the Reformation Doctrines of Justification." *Harvard Theological Review* 75, no. 1 (1982).

McGrath, Allister. *Historical Theology*. Malden, MA: Blackwell Publishing, 1998.

McGuckin, John Anthony. *The Orthodox Church*. Malden, MA: Blackwell Publishing, 2008.

McNeill, John. *Western Saints in Holy Russia*. Pasadena, CA: Mandate Press, 2002.

Melton, J. Gordon, and Martin Baumann. *Religions of the World: A Comprehensive Encyclopedia of Beliefs and Practices*. Santa Barbara, CA: ABC-CLIO, 2010.

Metzger, Bruce M., and Bart D. Ehrman. *The Text of the New Testament*. Fourth revised edition. Baker Exegetical Commentary on the New Testament. New York: Oxford University Press, 2005.

Meyendorff, John. *Byzantine Theology*. NY: Fordham University Press, 1987.

Meyendorff, John. *The Orthodox Church: Its Past and Its Role in the World Today*. New York: Pantheon Books, 1962.

Mohrmann, Christine. "How Latin Came to Be the Language of Early Christendom." *Irish Quarterly Journal Review 40, No. 159*, no. Sept (1951): 277–88.

Moo, Douglas J. *Galatians*. Grand Rapids: Baker, 2013.

Morris, Leon. *The Apostolic Preaching of the Cross*. Grand Rapids: Eerdmans, 1976.

Moss, C. B. *The Old Catholic Movement, Its Origins and History*. London: SPCK, 1948.

Mounce, Robert. *Romans*. The New American Commentary. Nashville: Broadman & Holman, 1995.

Muller, Richard A. *Dictionary of Latin and Greek Theological Terms*. Grand Rapids: Baker, 1985.

Murray, John. *Redemption Accomplished and Applied*. Grand Rapids: Eerdmans, 2015.

———. *The Epistle to the Romans*. New International Commentary on the New Testament. Grand Rapids: Eerdmans, 1977.

Nampon, The Rev. A. *Catholic Doctrine as Defined by the Council of Trent*. Philadelphia: Peter F. Cunningham & Son, 1869.

Nesmith, D.D., Rt. Rev. Michael. "The History and Beliefs of Old Catholicism." St. Michael's Old Catholic Seminary, 2004.

No author. *What Orthodox Christians Believe*. Ben Lemond, CA: Concilliar Press, 1988.

Olson, Roger E. *Arminian Theology*. Downers Grove, IL: IVP, 2006.

Packer, J. I. *Knowing God*. Downers Grove, IL: InterVarsity, 1973.

Pauck, Wilhelm. *Luther: Lectures on Romans*. The Library of Christian Classics. Philadelphia: Westminster Press, 1961.

Piper, John. *Five Points: Towards a Deeper Experience of God's Grace*. Fearn, Scotland: Christian Focus Publications, 2017.

Prokhorov, Constantine. "Between the West and the East." *Theological Reflections* 13 (2012): 79–105.

———. "Why Russian Baptists Are Neither Arminians nor

Toynbee, Arnold J. *A Study of History*. New York & London: Oxford University Press, 1961.

Trueman, Carl R. *Grace Alone, Salvation as a Gift of God, What the Reformers Taught and Why It Still Matters*. Grand Rapids: Zondervan, 2017.

VanGemeren, Willem. *NIDOTTE*. Grand Rapids: Zondervan, 1997.

Vedder, Henry C. *A Short History of the Baptists*. Valley Forge, PA: Judson, 1967.

Vickers, Brian. *Justification by Grace through Faith*. Phillipsburg, NJ: P&R Publishing Co., 2012.

Vine, W. E. "EDNTW." In *Work*. Vol. 4. Old Tappan, NJ: Fleming H. Revell, 1966.

———. "EDNTW." In *Justification*. Vol. 2. Old Tappan, NJ: Fleming H. Revell Company, 1966.

———. *EDNTW*. Old Tappan, NJ: Fleming H. Revell Company, 1966.

———. "EDNTW." In *Salvation*. Vol. 3. Old Tappan, NJ: Fleming H. Revell Company, 1966.

Walker, Williston. *A History of the Christian Church*. New York: Charles Scribner's Sons, 1970.

Walvoord, John F. *The Revelation of Jesus Christ*. Chicago: Moody Press, 1966.

Ware, Timothy. *The Orthodox Church*. New York: Penguin Books, 1993.

Weinandy, Thomas, and Daniel A. Keating, eds. *The Theology of St. Cyril of Alexandria: A Critical Appreciation*. London: T&T Clark, 2003.

Wenham, Gordon J. *The Book of Leviticus*. Grand Rapids: Eerdmans, 1979.

Westerholm, Stephen. *Justification Reconsidered*. Grand Rapids: Eerdmans, 2013.

Whitworth, David. "John Paterson and Ebenezer Henderson," March 2012. https://evangelical-times.org/23016/john-paterson-and-ebenezer-henderson.

Wilch, John R. *Concordia Hebrew Reader: Ruth*. St. Louis: Concordia, 2010.

Wilkinson, Bruce. *The CoMission*. Chicago: Moody Publishers, 2004.

Wunderink, Susan. "Faith and Hope in Ukraine: How Eastern Europe's Most Missional Evangelical Church Is Rethinking Tradition and the Great Commission." *Christianity Today*, October 2008. https://www.christianitytoday.com//ct/2008/october/25.70.html.

Zeleny, Igor. "An Analysis of Eastern Objective Soteriology." *Theological Reflections* 14 (2013): 66–90.

Zemek, George J. *A Biblical Theology of the Doctrines of Sovereign Grace*. Little Rock, AR: B. T. D. S. G., 2002.

"The Protestant Reformation exposed and corrected the false teachings of the Roman Catholic Church. As a result, there has been a clear doctrinal distinction between Protestants and Catholics. However, many Christians are confused about the Eastern Orthodox church which split with Rome in 1054 AD and has a stronghold in many Slavic countries today. Hal Hays sheds much-needed light on the teachings of the Eastern Orthodox church and provides a comprehensive treatment of the doctrine of justification by faith. This important volume is the fruit of his work, and I recommend it enthusiastically." – *John MacArthur, Pastor, Grace Community Church, Sun Valley, California; Chancellor, The Master's University and Seminary*

"After more than 20 visits to Russia and hundreds of hours of conversation with pastors and others from former Soviet regions, I used to think I had a good understanding of the Church History of the Slavic world. I had a rudimentary grasp of how Christians in that realm came to their doctrinal convictions. Then I read this book. My friend and colleague Hal Hays has given a great gift to all of us who seek to come alongside one another in the body of Christ across cultural boundaries. When I saw Appendix Four I realized what a precious treasure I held in my hands and what a debt I owe to brother Hal for gathering all this and explaining it so clearly. I will draw from this resource as long as God allows me to serve alongside my Slavic brothers and sisters, and I will encourage all who serve in such ministries to marinate their minds in its contents." - *Jim Harris, Pastor, Heritage Bible Church, Boise Idaho; Teacher, Heritage Bible Radio; Author of The Antioch Initiative curriculum of Slavic Gospel Association*